HELP! THIS MEETING SUCKS

How to Fix Bad Meetings, Reignite People and Performance.

PEG DRUMMOND

Here's to
great meetings
(it can happen)

Best,

Peg

Drummond, Peg

ISBN paperback: **978-1-988172-34-7**

 ISBN for eBook: **978-1-988172-35-4**

Printed and bound in the U.S.A.

Published by Norseman Books

Editing, illustrations, and cover design by Ingenium Books Publishing Inc.

www.superteams.com

*ATTENTION CORPORATIONS, UNIVERSITIES, COLLEGES AND PROFESSIONAL ORGANIZATIONS: Quantity discounts are available on bulk purchases of this book for educational or gift purposes, or for premiums for increasing memberships. Special book covers or book excerpts can be created to fit specific needs.

For more information, please contact Norsemen Books:

info@norsmenbooks.com

1-207-734-4950.

To My Mom

Meticulous bookkeeper.
Impeccable dresser.
Brought home the bacon,
and fried it up in a pan.
And without whom I would not be here.
Thank you.

To My Circle

(In alphabetical order)
Annie, Karen, Kelly, Kristine, Litza, Liz B., Liz L., Mo, Patty, Shelley, and Tim.
The cavalry, the goddesses, the warriors, my mothers, the Musketeers, the
sparklers and joy bringers, who teach me about true love and how to kick ass.

To My Children, Rose and Sam

For teaching me fundamental secrets to success in all arenas: listening, asking
open-ended questions, the profound beauty of time-outs and the generosity of
do-overs.

Contents

Introduction

Remember the last time you had to sit through a lousy meeting? You know the kind I'm talking about.

A meeting that starts late. Discussions that go off track. There's no agenda. What you were hoping to accomplish is lost in tangents. Frustration grows and personalities take over. Time is wasted—again—and the voice in your head is yelling, "Poke me in the eye! Get me out of here so I can go and get some *actual* work done." You might even spend time and energy thinking up tactics to get out of these crappy, ill-prepared, waste-your-time meetings. Sound familiar?

It's so commonly accepted that meetings will suck it isn't even a cliché anymore. It's the norm. It's spawned a whole industry of cartoons, mugs, stationery, and memes that attempt to put a humorous spin on this soul sucking ritual that happens in boardrooms and conference rooms across the globe every day over and over again.

Sadly, bad meetings are normal. I've been to meeting hell and back, and now I'm in the business of helping leaders, managers, and facilitators just like you find your way out of these meetings. And not surprising, my business is booming.

I have been facilitating and training teams for over two decades and people say to me, "Oh my gosh, our meetings suck! Help!" I've seen billions of dollars evaporate in projects that didn't come to completion. Not because of technical issues, or lack of expertise, but because the people side, which includes meetings, is impacting the business equation. Really smart technical experts say and do really stupid, oblivious things in meetings. Without clear and professional boundaries for behavior and communication, people don't commit. They leave action items undone. They are allowed to engage in condescending, shaming, and bullying behavior. They take over discussions, exude arrogance, and leave behind a trashy wake of hurt feelings and crushed relationships. In that environment, work does not get completed. At least not well. People don't care to go the extra mile. Morale, energy, creativity, and innovation and performance suffer. Good employees leave and look for other work.

It costs an organization 1.3 times an employee's annual salary to replace this person. Thirty percent more than the employee's annual salary. If the employee made $100,000 per year, it will cost $130,000 for the company to get a new person in and up to speed, when potentially the previous employee didn't have to leave in the first place. One rotating door leads to another, and another, as the main symptom driving your people away hasn't been addressed: what is happening in meetings that suck.

Meetings are where the people side of business comes together for planning, idea generation, and problem-solving. Being effective in the meeting arena doesn't happen magically. Yet many organizations and their leaders behave as though it does.

Why do great meetings matter? Meetings are the intersection between the people side and the technical side of your business. In a meeting with the right environment, human beings can showcase their talents and expertise. Most people want to perform well and be engaged in their work and have that work matter. Meetings are where it is possible for teams to collaborate and get work done. Most organizational functions overlap and intersect with other departments. We work as a system, not in isolation. Great meetings build relationships that last a lifetime and positively impact performance. They generate creativity and innovation.

Meetings are the petri dish that holds the health of your organization.

What happens in that one-hour weekly department meeting is a window into how the organization functions as a whole.

Bad meetings, at best, are like annoying rashes. They don't stop us from getting things done or living our lives. But they drain our energy little by little as we adapt to the itch. And boy can they get itchy, uncomfortable, frustrating, and annoying. So we cover them up, try some ointments to calm them down. When they get so bad that they can't be ignored, some savvy people will finally seek help.

For the most part, however, we let the problem continue. Why do we let these problems and complaints remain in place? We don't have to. We can stop the itch growing in the organizational petri dish right here, right now. Let's look under the microscope to uncover why your meetings suck, and what you can do about it.

Here's what you'll learn in *Help! This Meeting Sucks*.

Section I: Leadership Fundamentals

In this section you'll learn why and how organizational performance is tied to meeting performance. When you're facilitating a meeting, you *are* the leader, whatever your role is in the organization. We'll talk about the consequences—financial and otherwise—of bad meetings. I'll reveal the six most common blind spots. And I'll explain why meeting facilitation is a core competency of great leadership.

Section II: The Five Pillars

We'll take a deep dive into the components of great meetings and I'll provide suggestions to approach each one for best results. The five pillars are the session objective, the agenda, the agreements, the decision-making method, and the parking lot.

Section III: The Power of Prework

I devote an entire section of the book to prework. Prework covers all the things the great leader/facilitator does *before* the meeting to set up for success *in* the meeting. People plan for weddings and vacations months in advance, but rarely spend more than a few minutes preparing for a meeting. I'll explain why winging it is never a good strategy, and I'll walk you through the winning steps of prework, so you'll have awesome, productive meetings every time.

Section IV: Facilitator Superpowers

Here's where it gets fun. You'll learn the secrets of something so small and simple you'll be amazed by what a difference it makes. That's the gift of starting and ending on time, every time. Facilitator superpowers also include fluency with power questions, understanding and harnessing your energy, and emotional intelligence. And don't forget to set the tone using music. I've included a playlist!

Section V: Addressing Dysfunction

Section five is all about the tools that will let you navigate confidently even in turbulent weather. You'll learn how to flawlessly and seamlessly handle challenging personalities, including the storyteller, the pessimist or resister, the dominator, the bully, and the wallflower.

Section VI: Mechanics of a Great Meeting

We get down to business: preparation and set-up, opening the session (with scripts you can run with today) and effective exercises to help you and your teams get the most out of your time together.

Throughout the book I will either recommend or demonstrate things you can actually say as a facilitator. Instead of traditional dialogue format, what you read in *italics*, rather than "quotation marks," is what you could say out loud to your team.

This Book Is for You

This book is for you, whether you're a C-suite executive, a frontline manager, or mid-level leader. When you're facilitating a meeting—you're the leader.

Will my approach work? Ask Mike.

I was conducting a facilitation training session with a military division on the East Coast. Mike was a caricature of exactly what you would expect a military manager to look like: furrowed brow, crew-cut hair, rock-hard physique, and stocky even at six foot two. Mike kept speaking up during the session about what a difficult time he was having in his weekly meetings with the people on his team. People would come to the meeting and start talking about whatever was on their minds.

"We made up our agenda as we went along," Mike recounted. The meetings frequently went off track, and often devolved into gripe sessions. They rarely started on time, and whispering and texting throughout was common. Mike was at his wits' end and didn't know how to get his meetings under control. Scolding, calling people out by name, and giving them his "stink face" hadn't been effective.

We spent two days together discussing and practicing many of the key concepts you're going to read about in this book. Mike soaked it all up, nodding, taking notes, and contributing to the discussion and the hands-on exercises. But he had one nagging problem.

"I have no idea how I'll get the support of my operations manager to implement any of this," Mike said, leaning forward on his massive elbows. "I mean, I've asked him for support on how to get a handle on the people in these meetings, and he hasn't really been much help."

I asked Mike, "What do you think you could do to be sure your operations manager is briefed on what you've learned here today," I was ready to open up the floor to other training participants for suggestions, but with a little smirk on his face and a twinkle in his eye, Mike said, "Oh, that won't be a problem. He's sitting right over there." He pointed across the room at Bill, who was also smiling. It was clear this boss-employee relationship was a good one, and despite

Mike's concern about getting Bill's support, there was no animosity between these team members.

And Bill wasn't about to let Mike off the hook that quickly. Tactfully, Bill said, "Sometimes it's not just what's going on with the people in the meeting, it's the way the meeting is being facilitated. That has its own challenges."

"Agreed," Mike said, owning his facilitator role. "Bill, I'm going to do the steps and charts at our next big team meeting and you can give me your feedback!"

Mike and Bill both spoke with me during the next break. They were curious and concerned about how these new facilitation tools would work in the real world, especially with their difficult team. We brainstormed ideas to get Mike prepared since this meeting was coming up fast. Several days later at their next team meeting, Mike implemented what he had learned in our session and emailed me about the results.

"I was a rock star! This was so awesome. I used the charts just like you said, even though I didn't believe you; we stayed on track, got through our agenda and ended on time! It was the best meeting we had in months! I even had the team giving each other high-five's and fist-bumping, just like we did in training!" Mike also said Bill had thanked both him and the team for a great meeting. He was feeling on top of the world.

Bill emailed me as well.

"This stuff works! I could feel the sense of relief in that meeting room. There IS a path; there IS a way. We can get through tough conversations when it's organized, and there's been some thought put into it. We actually have action items and a timeline! I watched Mike use the facilitation tools we learned, and it has given me the courage to step up my own game now, too."

What I delivered in the training that made such a difference for Bill and Mike and the effectiveness of their team is what you're about to learn in this book.

The secret is so simple. Really. It's so simple to have great meetings, and to change your team's performance, engagement, and happiness. For the better.

Section I: Leadership Fundamentals

ONE

What's Growing In Your Petri Dish?

---

*A*s a team leader, you share the responsibility for the performance of your organization, department, and section. Every organization, regardless of industry or size, is made up of people. People get things done by—meeting. If you mistakenly believe that "it's just a meeting", your organizational performance will suffer. The negative impacts of bad meetings on your organization are far-reaching and expensive.

Meetings that suck are so prevalent that cartoons, TV shows and memes about them are constantly created to poke fun and gloss over the real frustration and pain, the loss of money and human potential.

Morale, creativity, innovation, and the engagement and enthusiasm of your people are smothered. Your organization may show the symptoms of inefficiency: being slow to innovate, collaborate, and adapt to market changes and customer needs. Your company's internal reputation suffers as employees vent their frustration in break rooms, hallways and cubicles.

And we know that in today's business world the best and brightest aren't sticking around long if they aren't being utilized to their fullest potential. Your company's reputation is broadcast to the world on social media and beyond as people leave for new positions.

Bad meetings affect your bottom line and profits. It's difficult and costly to recruit new talent, especially if your projects and initiatives aren't completed efficiently, or at all. With social media, news travels fast.

When you look at your business from thirty-thousand feet up, how many of the conflicts, the challenges, and the problems in your business are a direct result of the technical side of your business? How many problems are tied to the people who *do* the business? And, where does a lot of the business discussion get handled? In meetings. And yet, who hasn't heard story after story of people who want to poke their eye out to get out of another lousy meeting! How much time and focus is spent in your organization creating the environment for collaboration, creativity, and innovation to thrive? Those conditions don't happen magically. If meetings are a petri dish, a micro view of what's happening on a macro level, in your organization, what do you see when you look closer?

TWO

The Meeting Money Pit

*L*et's look at the cost, in dollars only, of your one-hour weekly team meeting.

Let's say there are 10 people. Each has an average salary of $80,000 per year which is about $40.00 per hour. They meet weekly for a one-hour department meeting: $40.00 x 10 people = $400.00 per hour.

That one weekly meeting x 50 weeks per year costs your business $20,000.00 per year.

Now, how many people do you know who attend only a single one-hour meeting a week? A lot of my clients and colleagues attend multiple meetings every day, at least five days a week. Managers spend about 30 percent of their time each week in meetings and think that over 50 percent of those meetings are a waste of their time. Ouch.

Back to our 10 people. Let's say they attend an average of 5 meetings a week.

$40.00 (hourly wage) X 10 (number of people) X 5 (number of meetings) = $2000.00 each week in salary costs alone.

Here's where the math starts to become staggering:

$2000.00 x 50 weeks = $ 100,000.00 spent on ten people attending one meeting a day for a year.

What if there are ten meetings a week happening in your business? With ten people involved? That's $200,000 per year.

Nearly a quarter of a million dollars—for one week's worth of meetings!

What if your organization has 20 people who attend 10 meetings a week?

$400,000.00 in a year. Now let's say 50 percent of them are a waste of time.

As you ponder the cost of bad meetings in your own organization, consider what we know to be true: out in the field, or just down the hall, most meetings start late, are unorganized, don't have an agenda, and frequently go off track. How much money is being flushed down the toilet?

And we haven't factored in the costs in terms of morale, creativity, innovation, trust, and respect. These are the intangible effects that drive people to leave your organization.

What could you accomplish in your business with that $100,000, $200,000, or $400,000 a year?

How do we get this math working in your favor?

THREE

The Culture Cost

See if you recognize the domino effect of bad meetings. One seemingly insignificant step tips into the next causing a chain reaction that ripples throughout the organization.

Domino #1: First-contact Compliance

Participants are "told" to show up at the meeting, typically via calendar invite or email, and aren't given much detail about it. The invite isn't particularly engaging or interesting, but the process is so familiar they are numb to it and comply. Some participants will accept the invite, some won't accept it but will still show up at the meeting. A classic nonverbal protest. "Yeah, whatever. I had to be here."

Domino #2: Why Am I Here?

People arrive at the meeting unsure why they are there or what their role is. Answering all these questions to clear up the confusion takes more time. Frustration begins to bubble along with more questions, skepticism, and low-level agitation. "God, I hope this isn't a waste of time. When are we going to get started?"

Domino #3: The Pack Hunts (aka The Facilitator as Food)

Let's talk science. Some mammals' exhibit pack behavior in certain settings. Lions, for example, come together to hunt. They communicate nonverbally as they assess who in the herd they're tracking is the weakest and easiest to take down.

Humans are a little like lions, at least in one respect. By starting your meeting late, being unprepared and unorganized and allowing discussions to go off track you begin to look like food—the wounded antelope. You trigger the primal pack-hunting behavior in your team. When a meeting facilitator/leader is not highly trained in facilitation skills, or is perhaps even lacking in emotional intelligence, participants sense vulnerability and close in for the kill.

Domino #4: Dysfunction Erupts

Personalities dominate to fill in the void left by the ineffective facilitator. As the pack assesses who is the alpha in the room, a range of dysfunctional behaviors can erupt, from texting and whispering to full scale revolt. If the facilitator takes little or no action to get the team back on track, or addresses the dysfunction ineffectively, behaviors can escalate. Participants and/or the facilitator may say things that are hurtful, condescending, or blaming. Frustration mounts for those not participating in the dysfunction, which breeds new kinds of dysfunction. In the vacuum they find other things to do: doodling, making their grocery list, taking calls. Without effective facilitation and leadership tools in his or her toolbox, the facilitator may revert to command-and-control tactics—the kind he or she may have seen modeled in school. For example (insert snappy, bad teacher voice), "Justin, Jen, why don't you share with everyone what you're talking about?" Or, "Mark, you're so quiet. Speak up! What are you thinking?"

Energy and engagement are squashed. Any hope of a productive discussion on the issues is slowed, stalled or at a standstill. It feels like everyone got on the bus to meeting hell.

Domino #5: The Hangover

The bad-meeting hangover leaves everyone feeling yucky, stale, low energy and sometimes nauseated. People report leaving meetings with headaches—even migraines!

If the meeting involved arguments, name-calling, or blaming, relationships will be forever impacted. Grumbling and gossip begin to spread. Other meeting hangover symptoms include comments such as, "Why did we have to sit through *that*? Whatever, could have been an email." Action items are rarely followed up on. People are left not knowing the status of next steps and their questions are left unanswered.

Domino #6: The Legacy

The legacy of a bad meeting can be serious. Problems remain unsolved. Projects aren't completed effectively and efficiently leading to a negative impact on overall company performance. You lose money. Frustration, venting and gossip increase. The focus of gossip becomes difficult people and personalities. The expectation bar is set low for future meetings, (e.g., stale and sloppy, and people learn it's okay to show up that way). Low morale and apathy begin to appear and attendance at meetings declines. There's an erosion of respect and trust. Communication between shifts, teams, departments and leaders is mediocre. Vital information isn't passed along the chain, leading to failures out on the production floor and in the field. The impact of poor communication is incredibly serious for businesses where safety in the field is an operational priority. In a hostile meeting environment, people don't speak up about what's really happening for fear of retribution, or at the least, looking stupid. Injuries occur. Fatalities can be a reality.

FOUR

Meeting Blind Spots

*K*nowing the consequences of bad meetings isn't always enough to change the culture and make meetings better. Why? Because of what I call "meeting blind spots." These are the attitudes and opinions about meetings that must be addressed first before great meeting skills can be effectively taught, learned, implemented and modeled. These meeting blind spots may be the root cause of the bad meetings that are sucking the life out of your business. How can you know what you don't know, or see what you can't see? These are the six most common meeting blind spots. Which do you recognize?

Blind Spot 1: Meetings Are Just Meetings. What's the Big Deal?

This blind spot ignores the fact that meetings that suck are a glaring root cause of underperformance, loss of talent, disgruntled employees, low morale, and missed business goals. Leaders continue to be promoted because of technical expertise, without regard for the skills required to manage the team on the people side of the business equation. They are unprepared and wing it—and it shows. This blind spot is contagious. When it affects the leadership and management of an organization, it spreads throughout the entire business. And the cycle of low expectations for performance in meetings continues.

Blind Spot 2: Our Meetings Are Good Enough. We've Heard About Worse.

It's interesting how many companies believe they run good meetings and how many people tell me what great facilitators they are. If no one speaks up and disagrees, and you don't hand out evaluations at your meetings I wonder what data you're using to measure your performance? I sit in on plenty of "good enough" meetings witnessing the results. An organized, efficient meeting is actually pretty rare. Half the time, people think they're doing great, and half the time they know they need some help. "But our meetings aren't a complete disaster." they say. "And besides, we've heard about those horrible meetings at that other company, and we're not that bad."

Blind Spot 3: Learning by Osmosis: We Just Need a Few Effective Meeting Tips.

If you're leading a team, you may hope that you've picked up some facilitation skills by osmosis along the way to help you run effective, efficient meetings. This is rare, and a bad strategy. Meetings and the projects they are designed to move forward rarely fail due to technical data or research. Projects and teams fail because the team falls apart on the people side. When you compare the money and time spent on training and developing employees on the technical side of a business with that spent on employees of the people side of the business, you'll usually find an equation severely out of balance. Managing other humans beings is a full-contact sport. We are complex, emotional, and unpredictable, and at work we're under pressure and stress.

Getting a few tips is not enough to rebalance the equation.

Blind Spot 4: Good Meetings Happen Naturally

While people high in emotional intelligence may be more skilled in managing the people side of a business, and are sometimes more natural facilitators, good meetings don't happen naturally. Even a *bit* of training is often not enough to make a *natural* facilitator effective. Some consider training to include reading pamphlets or reviewing computer-based programs. Caution: many of these programs or sessions are PowerPoint heavy and offer little hands-on practice. Imagine learning to play golf, throw a Frisbee, or ride a horse by watching a PowerPoint presentation or a video alone. Effective facilitation that results in great meetings is a special skillset that needs to be learned through coaching and feedback from an expert in this field; and it requires practice. Otherwise, it's so easy to model what we've seen others do, bad habits and all.

Blind Spot 5: Our Meetings Have Nothing to Do with the Organization's Performance.

A blind spot for leaders is an inability to see the connection between how their teams perform in meetings and how they perform in general. Remember, meetings are a petri dish of what's going on in the organization. Poor bottom-line results? Poor performance indicators? Poor customer-satisfaction scores? I'm waving the warning flag here: check the quality of your meetings.

Dysfunctional meetings equal dysfunctional teams. Dysfunctional teams underperform. Morale is low and people are unhappy. They do less than their best with your customers. They leave the organization in hopes of finding a better place to work, even if the salary is less.

Those who do stick around become so exasperated with the meetings that suck they start to act out. They come in at their worst, they're frustrated, and after years in this environment they finally lose their temper. Then they get a bad rap for blowing up at a meeting.

Blind Spot 6: We Have More Important Priorities for Our Training
Dollars.

How much money is in the training budget? And, how much money is
left over and up for grabs after taking into account the training that
must happen by law? It's a challenge for organizations.

I get it. Sometimes there isn't enough to go around and there are
no choices about how to spend your training dollars.

But in many cases you do have choices. What are you choosing?

It is the definition of insanity to keep doing something that is not
working and expect to get a different result. Bad meetings don't magically change to good ones.

Facilitation is a core competency of great leadership, so when I
hear decision-makers say, "We don't have time for that type of training," I hear the little voice in my head saying: "Blind spot!" It's ironic.
How can you afford *not* to get this type of training?

Meetings are where the work gets done. Or not. Being a leader, at
any level of your organization, does not mean you're a great facilitator.
However, great facilitators *are* great leaders. Test it out for yourself.
I've seen organizations dedicate one year to focus on changing the way
their teams work in meetings and then measure overall performance.
The results on the technical and the people side tell their success
stories.

FIVE

Facilitation = A Core Leadership Competency

*W*hen you're assigned the role of facilitator for a meeting or team, you simultaneously become the leader. Exceptional facilitation is a core leadership competency. Regardless of your role and rank on the technical side of the business, when you're leading a meeting and a team, your role on the people side is now your number one responsibility.

During facilitation and leadership development sessions, I prompt each team to think about great leaders they've known, real or imagined. We make a list of the qualities that make them great leaders. The list invariably includes the following words and phrases:

- Inspiring
- Trustworthy
- Audio matches video (i.e. they do what they say and say what they do)
- Great listener
- Asks questions
- Effectively resolves conflict
- Helps people with disparate views reach consensus
- Respectful of others' time
- Kind, caring, and empathetic

Interestingly, every single one of these qualities can be modeled when you're facilitating a great meeting. What an opportunity. On the other hand, simply being a leader doesn't automatically mean you're a great facilitator. Think about it this way: when a leader runs a meeting that sucks, you can take the qualities on the above list and turn them upside down.

- Uninspiring
- Untrustworthy
- Audio and video are out of sync
- Rarely asks questions
- Creates an environment for conflict
- Enters into conflict with others
- Unable to help others reach consensus
- Disrespectful of others' time
- Selfish, thoughtless, oblivious

Most of these qualities send the message that neither the meeting nor the team is important.

How inspiring is it for your team to see you unable to stick to a simple thing like starting your meetings on time? Why would your team trust what you say about bigger issues, when they can't even trust you to start a meeting when you said it would start?

You cannot hide when you're facilitating a meeting. Every meeting is a leadership boot camp opportunity. You're live and in real time. If you don't know what you're doing up there, you *cause* dysfunction. Your reputation is affected. People don't want to waste their time sitting through something that's of no value. Some leaders pick up on that—they know it's not going well, but they aren't sure why or what to do about it, so the problem continues.

Some leaders know they aren't doing well, and their fight-or-flight instinct kicks in or their egos erupt. They begin squashing people with their comments or take over in command-and-control mode: "Well, thanks for your ideas but this is what we're going to do anyway."

Doing so leaves the leader looking like a loser.

Organizational Retraining and Upping Our Bar!

How exactly do you go about changing the culture, the expectations and the behaviors around meetings? Here are my best tips for pushing reset on meetings that suck.

1. **Acknowledge the past.** Apologize for the history. "We want to improve how we perform as a team, and we can do that in how we handle our meetings. We know your time and energy have been wasted in ineffective meetings. We're sorry. That will change and we need your help!"
2. **Set best practices** and be clear about the WHY for each of them. Answer the question, "What's in it for me when we do it this way?" Here's a sample script. *We have used your feedback about what drives you crazy in meetings to develop a list of best practices. Our plan is to upgrade our meeting structure, implementing new tools to keep us on track and focused so you feel your time in meetings is well spent. Here's the list (insert your list):*
3. **Train facilitators** in the best practices.
4. **Identify how to hold people accountable** to the best practices. Communicate the rewards for success and what will happen and why if standards aren't met.
5. **Practice, practice, practice.** This will be easy—there are meetings every day!
6. **Measure the results.** Implement an evaluations process for every meeting. Course correct as needed.

The good news is that being a great facilitator/leader can be simple. It really can. Learning what it takes to run a great meeting is a critical place to start. Stay tuned.

Section II: The Five Pillars

SIX

The Session Objective

PILLAR ONE

*I*magine the Parthenon in Athens, Greece.

The giant white marble pillars are the foundation for everything the superstructure supports above. The architecture, over two thousand years old, is a testament to its design and function. In designing effective meetings, we replicate this superstructure with our own five pillars. They are posted on five charts at the front of the room wherever your meetings are held and become your foundation for taking action, keeping the team on track, and managing dysfunction.

This chapter provides an overview of them. Later, I'll show you how they work in action. As we move forward and define the five pillars of a great meeting, we'll be creating a common language.

The five pillars of every great meeting:

1. The session objective
2. The agenda
3. The agreements
4. The decision-making method
5. The parking lot.

Every successful meeting has each of these five pillars engaged. Every. Single. Meeting.

The Session Objective

 Begin with the end in mind.

Stephen Covey

Without a clear session objective, it's easy to be off track from the moment you start the meeting. Too often the facilitator/ leader doesn't identify this most important element in advance. Your session objective answers these questions: "Why are we here? What is the goal?" "What will we have accomplished when we walk out of this meeting?"

Examples of session objectives include the following:

- Provide updates on action plans and next steps
- Share information on new procedure and its impacts
- Team huddle: discuss this week's hot topics
- Improve the XYZ process
- Identify top-three actions for the next quarter
- Plan goals/objectives for one year (or, the next three years, five years, etc)
- Develop a team charter.

It's more common for the regular, one-hour departmental meetings to proceed without any thought given to the objective than it is for a two-day off-site strategic planning session. However, the one-hour meeting is just as important.

Here's a scenario I see frequently. A decision has been made at corporate head office or somewhere up the chain. It has been decreed change is to be made. The boss of the department is having a meeting to inform his team about this change. And he's winging it, because, well, because these meetings happen every week. So, he hasn't taken the time to really think through what the objective of the meeting is.

"Okay everybody," he says to the team, kicking off the meeting. "I wanted to talk with you about this upcoming change we've been told about that's on the horizon. What do you all think about it? Do you like it?"

Not surprisingly, the session turns into a discussion of the pros and cons of this change. Oh, let's be honest. Mostly cons. People don't like change. So the conversation starts to focus on why the team doesn't like it, why it won't work. The pessimists and resisters are dissecting the many ways this idea will fail.

The hour is nearly up when the boss realizes he's gotten completely off track. The bulk of the meeting has been spent disputing or agreeing with the many what-if's of this potential big change.

With a few minutes remaining in the meeting, the boss says, "Oh, I guess I should tell you, this has already been decided at corporate, and it's gonna start June 1."

A gasp is heard from the back of the room. As the team files out the door to their next meeting, they groan and look pained. If you could only hear their thoughts. Ouch.

What has the facilitator/boss just done? Without a clear session objective, he has taken the team completely off track and poked the hornet's nest. By default, the session objective became whether the team liked the idea or not. That entire hour of discussion was a complete waste of their time. The decision had already been made. They had no control over it. Not only did they spend an hour deciding they didn't like the change, but also, *surprise,* the boss blindsided them, wasted an hour of their time, and ticked them off.

If this sounds familiar, I'm sorry.

The good news: it doesn't have to happen again.

In this case, identifying the session objective in advance would have saved this team and the organization a whole lot of time and pain in what's now going to be a very bumpy rollout of this new initiative.

With a few minutes of prework, the boss could have clarified and decided why the team was meeting.

Session Objective: Inform team about new decision
Agenda:

- What's been decided (details about decision)?
- How does it impact the organization?
- How will it impact the team directly?
- What's in our control?
- What's not in our control?

If time remains, the boss could use the team's expertise to do the following:

- Create a list of potential challenges in implementing the new decision
- Determine how to mitigate those challenges
- Create an action plan for next steps.

To chart the most efficient route on a journey, first you need to know where you're going to end up. If the session objective is the destination, the agenda is your map to get there.

SEVEN

The Agenda

PILLAR TWO

*O*nce you've identified your session objective, you can move forward and build an agenda. Here is the bare-bones framework of a good agenda:

> *Welcome and overview*
> *(including the five pillars)*
> *Review and updates*
> *(info from/since last meeting, as needed)*

The body of the meeting will depend on the session objective.

> *Action planning*
> *Review and close*
> *(see steps for this later in the book).*

Here's an example of an hour-long department meeting agenda with the following session objective.

> **Objective: Update/clarify current actions and new business.**

Agenda:

1. *Welcome and overview*
2. *Review and updates (info from sub teams since last meeting)*
3. *New business (Ben—safety protocol, Kim—new training)*
4. *Action planning (determined by discussions in the meeting)*
5. *Review and close.*

Here's an example of an agenda with a different session objective.

Objective: Improve the hiring process.

Agenda:

1. *Welcome and overview*
2. *Review and updates*
3. *Current state: (What steps are in our current process? How do we do it now?)*
4. *Ideal/future state: (What do we want it to look like?)*
5. *SCOT: (Strengths, challenges, opportunities, threats)*
6. *Potential solutions*
7. *Creating the map*
8. *Action planning*
9. *Review and close.*

As long as you're clear on the session objective, there are options available in terms of the agenda steps to achieve it. Not sure what to include on the agenda? No problem. You don't have to figure it all out on your own. Engage the team early. The sooner they are a part of the process, the quicker they understand the project and their role in owning the results.

In fact, if you're not clear on the agenda for a large-scale meeting or project, dedicate time for a meeting with the following session objective: *Plan the most efficient agenda to achieve the session objective.*

There will be more on this in Section VI, Mechanics of a Great Meeting.

What Not to Include on the Agenda

Don't include times on the agenda (at least not on the version that will be visible to meeting participants). Of course you will have your working agenda all timed out, but the team doesn't need to see it. That's too much information for them. They'll start paying attention to timing rather than the topic. Build in ten- to fifteen-minute time cushions throughout your meeting. In a day-long session, round up your timing to give yourself an extra fifteen minutes for topics that will likely take forty-five minutes to cover. This gives you wiggle room for discussions that go longer than predicted, lets you control the cushions you've built in, and helps you decide when the breaks are actually needed. The perception becomes that you're always on time.

After the agenda steps are laid out, you can determine the best way to accomplish each agenda item. More ideas on that coming up.

EIGHT

The Agreements

PILLAR THREE

> The difference between the right word and the almost right word is really a large matter—it's the difference between the lightning bug and the lightning.
>
> Mark Twain

ords are power. Ask for what you want. It's common in meetings to call agreements "ground rules". We would like people to come to *agreement* in our sessions. The term "ground rules" can set a non-collaborative tone and serves to immediately, if subliminally, set up adversarial conditions in the room.

The Agreements

Respect the speaker
All ideas welcome
Freedom to disagree
Start and end on time
Electronics off

These five agreements cover every issue that comes up in a meeting.

I'm going to outline how to explain each of these agreements when you're leading a meeting. In the following section everything in italics is *your script*. I've removed words that could trigger conscious or unconscious reactions. You can make it simple for yourself by sticking to the script. It's your safety net when managing dysfunction throughout the session. (We'll talk more about preventing and managing dysfunction in Section V: Addressing Dysfunction.)

Book yourself an hour of planning time to begin to familiarize yourself with the script, then rehearse it out loud, in front of a mirror, so you're more comfortable using it with a live team. Here's an example of an opening script.

> *Here are our agreements, team. These are the ways we agree to work together while in this session to keep us on track and focused.*
>
> ### 1. Respect the speaker.
> *We'll agree to have one speaker at a time as a common courtesy. We can all do that, yes?*

(And everybody will say yes or nod.)

> *How many of you have ever been in a meeting where people were whispering?*

(Everybody raises their hands.)

> *There's a funny thing about whisperers.*

(Adopt a stage whisper.)

> *They think nobody can hear them because they are whispering.*

*But everybody hears them, right? And it's distracting. How
many of you agree to hold our whispering?*

(Shoot your hand straight up in the air and watch how many
quickly follow your lead.)

*Instead of whispering, just raise your hand and get that idea out
there. How would that be? Or, if you're not ready to shout it
out, use the sticky notes that you see on the table to write
down your idea. How would that be? It will help keep us
on track.*

(You'll usually get a few chuckles, and everybody will say yes.)

2. All ideas welcome.
*The more ideas we hear, the more potential solutions we will have.
In fact, those way-out-of-the-box ideas often become the spark
for solutions we may have never considered. So, please, when
you have an idea, put up your hand. Let's get all our ideas
out here.*

3. Freedom to disagree.
*With all these ideas out on the table, we may not agree with
everything we're hearing. It may not align with our
experiences, our values, or our belief systems. And that's
okay.
In my role as facilitator, one of my responsibilities is to make sure
participants can talk about anything in the meeting in a
respectful, professional way.
You can count on me to make sure we can talk about anything in
here. Conflict is good on a team. It's a sign that we're willing
to say what we really think. How does that sound to
everybody?*

4. Start and end on time.

We will start on time, at 9:00 a.m. We'll have a break every sixty
to ninety minutes. And we'll end on time, at 4:00 p.m.

(Insert your own times.)

If we seem to be running toward the eighty- to ninety-minute
mark since the last break, make two fists, put them thumb-
sides together, then break them in half. Let me know with this
signal that it's time for a break!

This lets meeting participants know that their engagement matters, and that you will respect their input and their own sense of when a break is needed

5. Electronics off.

There is nothing quite as disruptive to the flow of a good meeting than a ringing or buzzing phone. Conversation stops. And even if it doesn't, more than half the participants stop paying attention to what is being said, and start looking around to see whose phone is making the noise. This includes texting, surfing the web, looking at emails, Facebook or their computers. So, turning all electronics off is the fifth agreement.

How many of you have been at a meeting where electronics can be
distracting? (Hands go up.)
We don't want that to happen here. Make sense?
Great, go ahead and check your phones and turn them off for now.
Who here might be an emergency point person—someone who
needs to stay in touch with someone outside this meeting?
If this is you, would you please turn your phone to mute or
vibrate? And if you get a call, would you take that out in the
hall? Thanks.
For everyone else: here is the gift and practice of focusing like a

*laser. Please turn your electronics off and reconnect only
during breaks, Thank you so much!*

Solicit input from the group on whether there is anything to add to the list of agreements.

*How are these for us as a place to begin going forward? What
would you like to add? What comes to mind?*

Depending on the session objective, what's up for discussion, and who is in the room, it's not uncommon for "confidentiality" to get added to the list of agreements. This means what's discussed in this meeting stays in this meeting. If this is the case in your meeting, grab a marker and add it to the bottom of the list.

*Confidentiality. What we talk about in this meeting stays in this
room. How does that sound to everyone?*

(Heads nod.)

*That would also include not alluding to somebody everyone
knows. You might as well just say their name. Let's really
keep our game sharp and at a high professional bar. How does
that sound?*

These five (or six) agreements cover everything I've seen come up in a meeting. I've also been at meetings where there are twenty-five things on the agreements list. How can you, as facilitator, keep track of that? The answer is that you can't if you want to facilitate a great meeting. Keep it simple.

NINE

The Decision-Making Method

*I*ntact teams who have been meeting for a long time may have a decision-making process in place that is working for them. However, they may not have talked about it. You want to make it overt.

How does your team make decisions? What is their role in the decision-making process? In my twenty-plus years of facilitating meetings, large and small, I've used consensus decision-making as my number-one, most-reliable, best-results method.

I consider consensus to be decision-making through discussion rather than voting. In meetings I facilitate, consensus means this: "I, as a participant, can live with that idea/decision and support it." Consensus does not have to mean this: "I think this is the best/only solution."

The power of this method of decision-making is that it allows us to track concerns as important data while action and implementation still moves forward.

Rarely on a team will you get everyone loving a decision or idea at 100 percent. If a team can see some merit in the proposed path, *and* their concerns about this path are acknowledged and noted in the parking lot (our next pillar, Chapter 10) as "caution flags" during implementation, most teams can say yes to a decision and move forward into action planning.

Some teams get stuck and are unable to make a decision, believing everyone on the team has to love the idea or they can't go forward. Or, they believe that if someone has a concern, they can't move ahead. I've been told tales of teams that have literally been attempting to make a decision for years.

Defining the role to be played by the group is key to making decisions. Are they there as subject matter experts to give their opinion on a decision to be made by a smaller group, a leadership team, or the boss? Are they there to dissect the issue, weigh in on solutions, choose the path forward and implement the go forward plan? Be clear about what you're asking your team to do. The session objective will help you clarify this.

Helpful Clarifying Questions

What's the session objective? What are we here to do? Perhaps:

- Form an advisory board?
- Provide opinions as subject matter experts?
- Create a plan?
- Implement a plan?

What are we being asked to decide? Has a decision already been made? If yes:

- What is the decision?
- Timeframe?
- Budget?
- Team selection?
- Resources?
- Execution strategy?

If a decision has not already been made, do we need to consider:

- Timeframe?
- Budget?
- Team selection?
- Resources?
- Execution strategy?

You may also find it helpful to ask the group to address these questions:

- What is in our control?
- What is not?

You'll want to refer to an effective exercise I call 'Mission Control'. More on that coming up in Chapter 29.

Know how you will make decisions before you go into your meeting.

TEN

The Parking Lot

PILLAR FIVE

he parking lot is the last of the five meeting pillars. The parking lot is a storage unit, usually a flip chart (what I call an easel stand with chart pads) or a section of wall that's suitable for sticky notes. It's a place to contain the off-topic ideas that surface during a meeting. These are ideas that aren't aligned with the session objective or the agenda bull's-eye. Sometimes they hit the wall well wide of the target board.

The mind doesn't always work in a linear fashion. Ideas flow that may be tangentially related, or not. One of the big challenges as a facilitator/leader is keeping your teams on track when, for example, you're talking about how to improve a process and somebody remembers they've got to plan the company holiday party and blurts this out mid-meeting. Or they share an idea that may not seem related to the topic at hand. What do you do with that? Remember that "all ideas are welcome" is part of agreements. The parking lot is a great place to park those ideas, up front for all to see.

There's real power in acknowledging an idea by writing it down. If it's not written down, the idea generator may feel dismissed or embarrassed, and the facilitator becomes responsible for remembering to pick up that idea later. Save yourself time and energy. Get the team involved. Have people write their idea on sticky notes and post them. Or grab them when they're done writing and post them yourself.

What Gets Parked?

Anything that isn't related to the agenda item you're currently discussing gets parked in the parking lot.

Say you're discussing the current state of a process and someone says, "Right there, that's where the problem is! If we could just get around that..." The topic has now shifted to problems with the process when you're supposed to be talking about the current state of the process. Park it!

Here's what you can say.

> *Thanks for that idea. Checking in: we're making a list of how we do things now—the current state. Sounds like you've identified a potential problem? Yes? Okay. We'll be getting to problems with the process right here.*

(Refer to the agenda.)

> *How about for now, put that idea on a sticky note and we'll hold it in the parking lot. We'll come get it when we get to problems.*

Or, perhaps you're talking about problems with a process and someone says, "Here's what we can do to fix that. It would be so easy to . . . " You've just jumped to potential solutions. Park it!

> *Thanks for that idea. Checking in. We're making a list of problems. Sounds like you've identified a potential solution, yes? Okay. We'll be getting to solutions right here.*

(Refer to the agenda.)

> *How about for now, put that idea on a sticky note and we'll hold*
> *it in the parking lot. We'll come get it when we get to*
> *solutions.*

What if someone brings up an idea that isn't even near the agenda?

Let's say the session objective is to improve the hiring process. The agenda item you're currently on is "current steps in the process." Someone says, "Hey, when are we going to talk about recognition for long-term employees?"

Someone else may jump in with, "Hey, that's not what we're here to talk about."

> *Yes, duly noted. AND in our agreements, we agreed to "all ideas*
> *welcome."*

Note: you want to say "and" and not "but." "And" presupposes that two things can exist at the same time.

> *Brains percolate all kinds of ideas—as brains do. We can store*
> *any ideas that aren't on the bull's-eye in the parking lot for*
> *now. We'll take a look at the parking lot during our review at*
> *the end of the meeting. Then we can decide what to do with all*
> *the items. How does that sound to everybody?*

What happens if somebody wants to put something in the parking lot that doesn't actually fit anywhere? What if it's way off base and you can't see that is has any value? I just put it up there, and I recommend you do, too. It saves time. I place sticky notes and markers on the tables, so people can write their own ideas down. If they're sitting close to the parking-lot chart, I'll get them to put the note up themselves.

At the end of the meeting the team can decide how they want to address the items

The good news is that often these ideas get handled during the meeting. The issue was the timing of them.

Either way, before major breaks (e.g., lunch) and before you close the session, go to the parking lot, and ask the team the following:

- What are we going to do with these items?
- Have we covered this?
- When will we cover this?
- Who will take this item and follow up with us on it? How? And by when?

Often, an obvious person will take on a parking-lot item. If it's something to do with finance, a finance person takes it. In the meeting notes, keep track of who took the item and how they will update/follow up with the team, so that it doesn't fall through the cracks and get lost. Ideas in the parking lot often become part of the agenda for the next meeting. Let's say the idea doesn't fit with the session objective. The content doesn't even belong in that meeting. And yet, it was a solution that could change the world! You don't want to lose that. So, you say:

> *Who will to take this? And how will you follow up with the team about it?*

Now let's say you've run out of time. People are heading to the door and there are items left in the parking lot.

> *I'm going to roll up this parking lot, and I'll bring it back to the next meeting. At the beginning of our next meeting, how about we take ten minutes to look this over really well?*

The unfortunate thing about the parking lot is that it gets a bad rap, and here's why. Often it isn't used effectively. I've seen this happen: at the end of the meeting the facilitator takes the parking lot sheet, with ten or fifteen sticky notes containing people's ideas and questions, rolls it up, and throws it in the garbage. Talk about breaking trust! You've just lost the respect of your team and you won't be able to use the tool effectively again.

More commonly, items put in the parking lot aren't followed up on and get lost in the swirl of what everyone is already busy doing. So, when an idea is put on the parking lot, eyes roll, because based on previous meetings, you and the team know that nothing will happen with that sticky note.

Remember it's a parking lot, not an abandoned-vehicle dump site.

We've just covered the five pillars: the session objective, the agenda, the agreements, decision-making method, and the parking lot. Taking the time before your meeting to clarify each of the pillars—and how you will use them in your session—creates the foundation for success in your meetings.

Section III: The Power of Prework

ELEVEN

Prework

> *Failing to plan is planning to fail.*

Dwight Eisenhower.

*W*hy do people start planning for weddings or vacations months and months—sometimes a year—before the event? Because they want to make sure their dreams come true? Well, yes, *and* they want to have time to handle all the details and correct course if needed. What if you applied that same rationale to your meetings and projects?

What Is Prework?

Prework is everything the facilitator does *before* the meeting to set up for success *in* the meeting. The prework process includes both sides of the project or meeting: the technical side, and the people side.

Depending on the type of meeting or project you're leading, prework can take just a few minutes (e.g., prework for a weekly department meeting) or it can begin months in advance (e.g., prework for a project launch). Regardless, the same five key steps are employed.

The five steps of prework:

1. Identify the session objective
2. Adopt a sales and marketing mindset
3. Pick the A-team
4. Invite and welcome the team
5. Order the coffee (and other logistics).

Most people don't do prework. It's not even on their radar. Instead, they wing it. Winging it is not a solid strategy for success and it shows. Here is a familiar meeting-911 call I get from clients who have been through one of my training sessions: "Help, I'm on a break and this meeting is a train wreck."

"Okay, tell me about the prework. What did the team know coming into the meeting?"

Silence. Then, "I didn't really have time to get to the prework. Everybody got a meeting notice about the upcoming change occurring."

"What about the charts: session objective, agenda, agreements, consensus, parking lot? What charts do you have posted?"

"Oh, right, I forgot to do that."

Unfortunately, it's not uncommon to spend the first half hour or more of a meeting figuring out all the stuff that didn't get handled because no prework was done. "Why are we here? Why are we doing this? Nobody told me this. I just got an email telling me to show up at this thing. What is this about? What am I supposed to do?" Your omission creates the environment for charged emotions and personalities. The team members don't want their time wasted, again.

When the facilitator/leader hasn't done the prework and is disorganized, or unprepared, everyone on the team is a witness to it. It sends a message that the team and the meeting or project aren't a priority and weren't worth the time to get ready for. Ouch. Count on that impacting the team's behavior.

Prework Prevents Dysfunction

You will spend at least as much time, if not more, cleaning up the messes created by not doing the prework as you spend doing the prework. The fallout of not doing prework can be daunting: damaged relationships, a tarnished reputation, and lack of interest in the project.

If you aren't in the habit of doing thorough prework, you may not understand its power and how it actually helps to save time and prevent dysfunction. Most organizations don't understand the time and energy it takes to do the prework well, or that dedicated planning time is required. Adopting prework as your standard approach to every meeting is the single most powerful change you can make to improve the quality of all your meetings.

Imagine this scene.

You arrive at your meeting. People are early, and they're excited, smiling, and curious. You hear music playing in the background and smell fresh-brewed coffee in the air. The meeting starts right on time! Team members are prepared for the discussions. They've accomplished the tasks assigned from the previous meeting and are looking forward to seeing how ideas are turning into tangible actions as the team moves forward. Everyone stays focused and engaged. You make it through the agenda with enough time to review the parking-lot items. And, with big high five's all around, the meeting ends right on time. Meetings can be strategic and effective and energized. It just takes prework.

TWELVE

Identify the Session Objective

*K*nowing where you want to go makes it a lot easier for you to get there. Most of us don't have the time or the money to start in New York City and head west on a cross-country road trip without a specific destination. Yet we do this, metaphorically, in our meetings and with our teams all the time. We aren't sure where we're going, how much time it will take, or why are we're even going on this trip. And we wonder why people get frustrated.

Remember, the session objective answers these questions: "Why are we here? What is the goal? What will we have accomplished when we walk out of this meeting?" The session objective is the bull's-eye on the target.

There are good reasons to get a team together. Be sure you know yours.

If you don't know *why* you're having this meeting—don't have it yet! You're probably not ready, and if you proceed, you'll be wasting your team's time and harming your reputation.

Before you schedule your next meeting know your why. Why are you asking people to leave their already-full plates and come to this meeting?

Ask yourself:

- Is it a weekly/bi-monthly face-to-face meeting to engage and support our team?
- What is the benefit to us as a team to meet face-to-face?
- What information needs to be shared in a face-to-face meeting?
- Are we here to make a decision? What is it?
- Do we need subject matter experts to weigh in with information that others will use to make a decision?
- Do we need to discuss the merits/challenges of new decisions and actions to be taken?
- Are we here to improve a process?
- Are we engaging in longer-range strategic planning?

If you're still not clear about your session objective after going through the questions above, you may need clarification from subject matter experts. Ask your team:

- Why are we meeting?
- What do you see as our session objective?

You may be surprised by what you hear.

Here's another common scenario. You find yourself as a team lead on a new project. Taking the time to be absolutely clear about what you and your team are being asked to do is imperative. It's not uncommon to find that the person who assigned you this role, maybe your boss, doesn't know the session objective either. Someone up the chain told this person to get the project started. While this can require some finesse, continue investigating until you're clear, or you may be off course before you begin. This is why prework is so important—and can take time.

Beware of Habit Meetings

There can be great value in getting the team together to check in, but make sure both you and the team can identify the value. Otherwise, you may be guilty of holding "habit" meetings. "We *always* have a meeting on Tuesday mornings at eight. That's our why. And, there are great donuts!"

Those weekly departmental meetings can begin to look like this. The first fifteen minutes of the meeting are spent getting settled in and deciding what to talk about. Who wants to go first...?

At worst, no one is quite sure why they are there. The facilitator wings it and starts talking to fill the vacuum. Since it feels like anything is open for discussion, gripe sessions begin.

If this sounds at all familiar, you may want to check in with your team.

> *Hey everybody, we have this weekly meeting. What value does it bring us?*

Maybe you'll discover that a meeting every other week would be enough.

Here's an example of clarifying the session objective.

A newly formed process-improvement team was looking for ways to make things easier, safer and more efficient at their plant. Where could they find a relatively easy win that would make things better for their business? This team was smart and went directly to the subject-matter experts. They began by walking around and talking to people out on the floor. "What's the biggest pain in your butt when you're trying to do your job? What gets in the way? How could it be easier?"

Here's one of the problems they heard a lot about. "We've got these huge hoses all over the floor. Because of what we do, we've got to have these hoses out. But you can see they're tangled up. They're all over the production floor. It's a mess. People trip. We had a guy fall and break his wrist two months ago. We've got to figure out something else to do with these hoses. How to store them, how to make them easy to get to, and how to keep them untangled."

This became their easy win.

The session objective: improve the flow and management of hoses. From there they could build the agenda to accomplish the objective.

THIRTEEN

Adopt a Sales and Marketing Mindset

*S*etup equals results. It's *how* we set up and engage the team that makes *all* the difference in the results we get. *How* we talk about the project or meeting, the reason it's a good idea, and the results we're looking to achieve set expectations for performance and affect how the team creates those results. From the beginning of the process of preparing for your meeting you will be interacting with people. This is where the sales and marketing mindset begins.

Pushback and Resistance

A large metropolitan county government was implementing a multi-year process-improvement initiative. Every department in the county system was going to be affected by this redesign and rollout.

"We're having terrible trouble implementing," said the project leader. "Nobody wants to come to our meetings. We get all this push-back and resistance."

"Bring me up to speed," I said. "Tell me about how you marketed your meeting. How did you tee people up for this huge change that's going to happen to them?"

"What do you mean?" Deer-in-the-headlights look.

"Well, what's happened so far? Let's look at the meeting notices you've sent out by email."

Subject line: Business Improvement Initiative

Hi everyone, per our long-range strategic planning process, it's
  been decided to upgrade, improve and change our system of
  doing business. All departments will be affected at some level.
  Please come to this information meeting to learn how you will
  be impacted.
Date, time, location.
/R.

It's not surprising that meeting attendance was low. Nor that they experienced a lot of resistance in the first few meetings, and that they spent a lot of time answering questions woven with frustration, confusion, emotion, and concern. The team lead's inbox was swamped with emails containing the following: "What the hell is going on? What is this about? Why are we doing this? Who decided this was a good idea?" Discussion and venting disrupted other meetings throughout the organization as people filled the void with speculation and gossip.

Many team leaders have this experience. They spend the first meeting trying to put out fires they created by *not* doing the prework. Prework *prevents* dysfunction.

Our work was to refocus and correct course. The planning team was wide open to ideas, given that their first attempt at this roll out was not going well. For the project to be successful, they needed hundreds and hundreds of employees to be open-minded, interested and prepared for a major change. This wasn't the way they wanted this project to begin.

First, we focused on increasing the planning team's facilitation and leadership skills with training and coaching. From that foundation we began to reboot their prework. In particular, we created a compelling sales and marketing piece to get the organization curious about and engaged in the project.

Several scheduled meetings were put on hold until thorough prework was completed, session objectives were nailed on the bull's-eye, and an apology ("Can we please have a do-over?") email was sent.

The planning team had many aha moments as we developed their sales and marketing plan for the project. They could easily see their former blind spots and how they were actually causing their own problems and creating dysfunction. Connecting a compelling, eye-catching email message to the people you want to become interested in your product (the meeting) is the business of sales and marketing.

Put on your sales and marketing glasses so you don't miss this often overlooked opportunity to get people on board fast.

We're constantly bombarded by advertising on the web, TV, radio, and billboards.

How would you create an engaging invitation, rather than a dull "accept or decline" order, to attract customers (i.e., teammates) to your meeting or team? Consider the following, and remember the basics:

Thanks for taking the time to read this email.

- What is the meeting about (session objective)?
- Why is it important? How will accomplishing the objective make things better, easier, faster?
- Why them? What is the area of expertise that makes them a candidate for this team?
- What are they being asked to do? What will be their role and responsibilities?
- What is the projected time commitment?
- How will they follow up with you about ideas and questions? (Provide your email, phone number, etc.)
- What are the logistics (time, place, what to bring, refreshments provided, etc.)?

Here's an example of a recently-sent email to a new team:

Subject line: Opportunity. Need your expertise!

Hi (name),

We're excited to invite you to be a member of our team!

The project is (overall objective) and what we're looking to create is (...)

You're being invited to participate because of your expertise in (...)

What's in it for you and why this project is important:

You'll be a part of a well-organized and efficient team. We will thoughtfully look at the X, Y, Z, process and consider ways to improve it for everyone's benefit so you can work safer, work faster, and get home on time!

My role: I will make sure we stay on track and focused in the meetings.

We'll have team agreements, so we can work together effectively.

We'll be making decisions by consensus. This means that based on what we're hearing and learning, we'll make sound decisions for next steps as a team.

Your role: bring your experience and what you know as a subject-matter expert to our meeting to discuss and make decisions.

Estimated time commitment:

How we're getting started and where we're headed:

(Insert what you know so far—first meeting, etc.)

Thanks in advance for your time and for considering being a part of our A—TEAM!

Please contact me with questions you have.

When could we meet for a quick fifteen-minute chat in person or by phone so we can talk about questions and ideas that you might have as well as to get you up to speed on the project?

Looking forward to talking with you!

For our success,

(Name)

We're focusing on the people side of your business here first. How do people like to be treated? How do we get their attention?

Sales and marketing of your meeting begins in the prework. Opportunities to market your work continue daily. Turn your radar on high. Listen to how you talk about your team, your department and your project. What kind of advocate and salesperson are you? What kind of results are you getting?

San Francisco Fiasco

I'd been hired by a multi-national company to facilitate a worldwide global check-in, strategic planning, and goal-setting meeting. The two big bosses, I'll call them Roger and Sam, were kicking off the session from Australia. I was facilitating in San Francisco. There were teams meeting at the same time in spots around the world, and we were all connected via video link.

The meeting started with Roger and Sam welcoming everyone and thanking them for taking the time to attend and for contributing their important ideas to the strategic goal-setting day. They outlined their high-level strategic goals and where they wanted the company to be at the end of the year. They wished us good luck and a great session.

Next up on the agenda, all the regional managers, on-site with their own teams, were to say a few words.

I knew that Roger and Sam expected each regional manager to say something appropriately inspirational. So, a few weeks before the big day, I set up a meeting with Justin, the regional manager in San Francisco. As facilitator of the San Francisco session, I wanted to be as helpful as I could, and I wanted to have some idea of what he planned to say.

"What have you been thinking about the meeting so far? What's your plan for the kick off? How can I help?" I sat across from him, the big walnut desk gleaming between us.

"Hey, hey, hey." Justin shook his head, waving me off as though I were a bothersome pest. "Don't you worry about it. I do this all the time. I've got it covered."

Okay, I thought. We'll see how this goes.

On the meeting day, after the powerful and inspirational opening from Roger and Sam, Justin stood up in front of the San Francisco team. Forty-five people had come from all over the western half of the United States for this day-long session.

"Wow. Roger and Sam, huh. Well, that was nice. You know, I don't really know why they're thinking of doing this. It's a cute, trendy, little idea. I'm skeptical, spending this kind of money and time, but we'll see where it goes. Um... well... we have some good lunch coming."

And with a caustic, "Have a nice day," Justin left the front of the room.

Silence. Stunned, confused, and agitated looks shot around the room, The bottom dropped out of the room's energy. Justin had left a dump truck's worth of crap all over the floor, and I was left with the shovel.

To this day I don't know if Justin had any perception of how disempowering and disturbing his message was. I do know that he didn't understand the value of the prework sales and marketing component. He had an opportunity to inject enthusiasm, to highlight the value of the team's impending contributions, to make them feel a part of something bigger. And he blew it.

The prework email is a key step. It's both a welcome and an invitation. It's an invitation even when the person *has* to be on the team. It's nice to be invited. It sets up a respectful environment as a foundation for the team. It answers questions and reduces confusion about what the project is about and it clarifies everyone's role, including yours as facilitator. It lays out the objective for the meeting, the why, and begins a healthy communication loop, opening the door for people to contact you if they have additional questions.

When you adopt the sales and marketing mindset, your team will arrive for the first meeting ready to go. They'll know why they are there, and what to expect. The energy and tone will be more upbeat and energized. There will be less resistance, less time wasted. And the discussion will be more thorough and productive.

FOURTEEN

Pick the A-team

O nce you're clear on your session objective and have a sales and marketing message, the next step is to identify the best team to achieve that objective. Sometimes you'll have the luxury of being able to pick your team. Sometimes it will be obvious who you need to have on the team. And in some cases the team is picked for you, or limited by workload, etc., and you get the team you get. When you do have the ability to choose your team, understand that the time and effort you put in during the prework phase will be well spent. Remember, you'll either spend your time setting up for success by doing your prework, or you'll spend at least the same amount of time —if not more—cleaning up the messes that happen in the meeting(s) because you didn't do your prework.

Caution! The Icky Secret

If you don't do your prework around team selection, you risk getting people whom departments want *out* of their office. You get their dead weight. "Get Bob out of here because he's such a complainer anyway. It will be a relief to have him out of the office once a week for these meetings." It's not uncommon for these kinds of people to get offered up.

Your "picking the A-team" prework begins by talking to people. Actually walking around and talking to others face-to-face.

Who are the best and brightest available to fill the roles you need? And how do you find them? Here are some ideas to consider.

Identifying the A-team:

- Who needs to be at this meeting and why?
- What value does this subject-matter expert bring to help accomplish the session objective?
- Who is perceived as a leader by their peers?
- Who is optimistic, with a can-do attitude?
- Who gets things done?
- Who finds a way around hurdles?
- Who is the creative problem-solver?
- Who is open-minded? Kind?
- Who is technically savvy?

Ask your team who fits the criteria in the list above.

When you have a list of potential A-team members, go talk to other leaders in the organization, the people who know or perhaps manage the people on your list. Update them about what you're trying to accomplish using your sales and marketing techniques from the previous chapter.

You may not always get the team you think you want. And, you may be surprised with the team you get. I've seen someone who is perceived as a problem flourish in a well-run facilitated environment with clear boundaries and expectations. They show up better because the professional bar is set high. The environment is respectful. The so-called problem person, along with the rest of the team, sees that the meetings and the project are organized and efficient. They respond to the request to contribute. Their ideas are heard and used to implement a plan that actually comes to fruition. A great team and a great meeting can change people. Be willing to be surprised!

Interviewing the Team: The Prework Begins!

It's best if you can meet with the potential members face-to-face. If not, interview them by phone. In these interviews, you'll get a sense if they're A-team or not. You'll uncover information that will guide you in planning next steps for your meetings.

Often, the A players carry a big share of the workload just because they're more efficient. They're probably tagged on a number of teams because they're high performers. It may be that adding them to your A-team would overload them. In an interview, you will be able to determine this. So, the interviews are critical to make sure you get the right people on the team from the start.

Interviews With Potential Team Members

1. Send out email invitations to the potential A-team members. (Remember your sales and marketing!)
2. Conduct interviews. In person is ideal, by phone is next best. Usually fifteen minutes as a first meeting works great. You can use this script as a guide.

> *Hi! Thanks for your time.*
> *What questions do you have so far?*
> *What's been your experience being on teams like this?*
> *What are your concerns about the project (so far)?*
> *What are your concerns about being on the team?*
> *Here's what we know so far (session objective, time commitment,*
>   *travel requirements, roles and responsibilities).*
> *How's this sounding to you?*
> *How do you see your experience and expertise fitting with this*
>   *project and this team?*
> *What is your advice for me in my role going forward?*
> *What else would be helpful to know?*

What happens if you do your interview and discover someone is not going to be a good fit? It happens. And there is a way to break up without hurting feelings. Here's what you can say (either in person or on the phone):

> *I've got some good news—you're off the hook for the XYZ project. The bad news: we'll miss you! Considering everyone's schedule, availability, and workload, as well as our budget, it looks like you won't have to be pulled away from your work. However, I'm wondering if I can call you from time to time with questions that might come up in your area? Thank you so much for your time.*

Interviewing team members and potential team members helps you do more than identify who is appropriate for your team. You can also find out the following:

- Who doesn't like where the meeting or project is headed
- Who feels that the session objective will impact them or their department negatively
- Which teammates may not get along, either personally or professionally

With the answers to these questions, you can develop mitigation strategies. Without these prework interviews, you're going into the meeting or project without the full set of team data you need. Save yourself time and heartache by setting yourself and the team up for success—do the prework interviews.

FIFTEEN

Invite and Welcome the Team

*I*n Chapter 13, you adopted a sales and marketing mindset to create email invitations for potential A-team members. Chapter 14 provided the path for selecting and interviewing your ideal team. Continue building strong communication with the people on your A-team by following up after the interview with both a "thank you" and a "welcome." Feel free to type the email below into a document you can keep and use in the future.

Hi (name)
I appreciate your time on the phone in our interview and I'm so
*   glad you're a part of the team!*
Here's what we've clarified so far:
Our team is: (team roster.)
Our next/first meeting: date, time, location.
Please arrive early to get a cup of coffee and get tucked in. We'll
*   be starting right on time!*

Session objective:
Agenda (for the next/first meeting)
Agreements:
Decisions by consensus: (give definition)

We're excited to get started!

We'll be having coffee and tea in the morning and finish up
*   with lunch.*

What would you like for lunch? Any allergies, likes, or dislikes I
*   should know about?*

Thanks for your expertise and support!

For our success,

(Your name)

With this kind of prework communication right from the beginning, surprises are minimized. You begin building an environment of trust, respect and openness. People feel their time is being valued before the meeting even starts. This affects how they show up as well. When people understand what they're supposed to do, the context of what they're doing, and the expected outcome, they walk in better prepared, less anxious, and ready to perform.

Without this kind of prework, communication gaps create confusion and breed dysfunction. Gossip and hearsay bubbles up based on people's history of attending meetings that have sucked. When people aren't clear about what they're doing or why they're attending, meetings and projects get off to a rocky start. The dominoes start tipping. The little voices in their heads are saying, "Oh boy, here we go again. Is this going to be another big waste of time?"

The more you can do to clarify what you know with your team, the fewer questions you'll leave unanswered. Which means they'll show up better prepared, better able to do the job they're there to do. And this means better project results.

SIXTEEN

Order the Coffee

---

*A*s facilitator, you may be responsible for the practical details around your meeting. Even if you're not, it's important to have a clear idea of what's involved with prework logistics, so you can support those who are.

Book the Best Room—Early

It was a hot sunny day. The door had been unlocked early so we could get set up an hour before the meeting began. As we opened the door, we were hit with a giant wave of humidity and a thick musty smell.

Then the cockroaches. Dead ones, as big as your thumb. They were littered along the perimeter of the indoor—outdoor carpeted floor. Ummm. My colleague and I, speechless, looked at each other.

A few moments later our contact arrived, apologetic. She explained she meant to book a different room, but forgot. And now, this was all that was left.

Oh, and by the way, around 10:00 a.m. the contractors will arrive to repair the air conditioner.

Were we wishing we'd booked the room early, so we wouldn't be stuck with this one? You bet.

Environment overrides willpower. Distractions take all forms, and a funky room can negatively impact the best team. Room too hot? Room too cold? Room too small? Bad sound system? Finicky or difficult computer hook-ups and log-in? Bathrooms too far away? Cockroaches? You'll lose people at the break and increase the likelihood they'll return late. Room configuration not flexible? You won't be able to choose the best seating arrangements for the session objective, team, and project. A room that has no options will cramp your style.

Room Set-up

Your agenda becomes a guide for how to set up the room. How many people are attending your session? What kinds of work will they be doing? Engaging in discussions? Brainstorming ideas? Let the work guide the set up.

What does a good room setup look like?

U Shape

I consider the U-shape best for groups between six and thirty people, for a variety of reasons.

1. Everybody can see everyone else, which enhances communication.
2. There's no second row where people can disappear, start whispering, or walk out.
3. The playing field is level, as all seats are in the front row.
4. Group work is easy in a U. You can break into small teams or partners easily.
5. It keeps participation and idea generation high.
6. It's easier to hand out materials.

As facilitator, you can manage dysfunction simply by walking in and out of the U. (More on this technique coming up in Chapter 22.) If you can't do a U, or you have more than thirty people, there are other options for room set-up.

Small Group Tables or Rounds

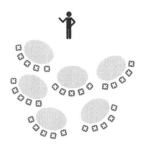

Chevron

If people aren't comfortable in their work setting, they get distracted. Discomfort and distraction make it harder to do work.

Some facilitators say, "We only have rooms with conference tables and they're bolted right in the middle of the room." What do you do? This is where you get creative.

If the room is large enough, and the conference table is not bolted down, take the table out of play. Instead, put chairs in a U shape (without a table) in the space available around the perimeter of the room.

This may disorient people. "Where do I put my stuff? Why are we doing this?

Smile and reassure them.

Feel free to set your gear on the conference table or over there on the chairs near the wall.

You'll get a sense of how teams view change, and of their adaptability to it.

If you can't take the conference table out of play, be sure to claim one end of the table as your front. Walk around the table to the opposite end as discussions are happening.

In our work as facilitators we do the best we can. Sometimes you get lemons, so make lemonade!

Refreshments

What's your budget for this? Coffee, tea, and water in the morning is a good way to start. Lunch and/or snacks in the afternoon are ideal especially for-kick off meetings where new teams are meeting for the first time. Are there dietary considerations? (You will have included this question on the welcome email, right?) Who is a reliable caterer? Contact them ASAP.

You might wonder why refreshments are important. Aren't we all there to work? Trust me: if you've got people in a meeting all day and no one ordered lunch, or the lunch count is wrong, it affects the team's ability to think. Many people take their lunch at nearly the same time every day. When that time comes around their body is ready for food. Stomachs override brains.

I was facilitating an international safety summit for forty-five people. The meeting location was shifted on day two, and the logistics person forgot to let the caterer know. Lunch was delivered to the original meeting room. There was another team meeting in that room.

They thought the lunch was for them and ate it. We had forty-five hungry people and an agenda that was timed for a working lunch because people were leaving for the airport early. It was a pretty big mess.

Luckily, the foundation for the summit had been laid with thorough prework. The meetings were on track, focused and energized. The lunch "miss" was seen as an obvious exception to a valuable session. (Another example of how important doing your prework can be.) Good will and professionalism prevailed on the team. Pizzas were delivered and the session went on smoothly.

If there isn't a budget for food, consider asking the team about the idea of a potluck. Food can be a great way to build community on a team.

Facilitator Care and Feeding

Don't forget about the care and feeding of you, the facilitator! Take care of yourself. You'll want to be at 100 percent. Make sure you've got water up there. In fact, bring extra. Be mindful of the fact that you need to be high energy through the *entire* meeting. Know what foods feed you and what tires you out. Your energy level sets the pace for everybody else.

Consider not eating the lasagna at lunch. All those carbs will kill your energy. It's better for the whole team if you can offer lighter options for lunch (e.g., salad with grilled chicken).

Other Logistics Considerations

- What else needs to get handled in the meeting room itself?
- Who is the point of contact for an off-site location?
- Who will unlock the meeting room door in the morning and how do you lock up at night?
- How will easels and chart pads be made available?
- Can you use tape on the walls?

- Who is responsible for AV support?
- How do you adjust the heating and cooling in the room?
- How do you evacuate the room in an emergency and where should everyone gather?

I'll go into more detail about logistics, supplies, and the step-by-step approach to facilitating a great meeting in Section VI: Mechanics of a Great Meeting.

Section IV: Facilitator Superpowers

SEVENTEEN

Power Questions

---

*I*magine that you're the best facilitator in the universe, a super hero among facilitators! You have forded deep and rushing rivers of exasperating discussions, agilely tiptoed across beds of oozing-hot-lava negotiations, and expertly brought divisive teams through thick, tangled jungles safely into clearings.

As you ready for your next adventure with a new team, you open your super facilitator golden toolbox, reach in, and take hold of your most prized tool for this session.

What is the one thing that can change your meetings—and even people's lives?

Your most powerful tool as a facilitator is the *question*.

One of the key differences between good and great facilitators involves communication. Great facilitators and leaders ask *lots* of questions. Questions hook the mind, and engage and involve the team.

Leaders want to hear from their team, learn what is really happening day to day in the field and understand how to support them (e.g., clear obstacles and run interference for them.)

How do they find out this critical information? They ask questions.

The questions you ask and the way you ask them can tap into your team's creativity and spark the innovation to develop new solutions and products. They can free your team from perceived constraints and help them leverage their years of experience to solve problems.

Our objective, as facilitators and as leaders, is to have the *team* do the work! It's not to have the team sit and listen to us go on and on while we reference our PowerPoint presentation. Snore.

If you ask a group of people to leave their work, to turn away from their already-overflowing plates and sit in a room with you, involve and engage them immediately. Turn the discussion over to the team as soon as possible by asking questions.

Asking questions:

- Invites participation
- Taps into the team's experience, skills, and creativity
- Helps to uncover solutions that are understood and accepted by the group
- Contributes to people feeling valued and respected.

The Trap: Telling Versus Asking

Facilitators are often trapped in the *telling* habit. They don't know what else to do. The telling approach to communication is a familiar model to many of us. We saw it when we were young, and continue to see it now, in our work lives. In many cases, it's what other leaders model for facilitators who are developing their own leadership style.

If you haven't had the coaching, training, or the time to practice doing something else, you may be in default mode, relying on habits that can have negative effects on your team, personally and professionally.

Many leaders are undertrained in how to engage and communicate with their teams—the people side of business.

How do you know if you're in the default *telling* mode with your team? Look for meeting-fatigue syndrome.

Meeting Fatigue Syndrome

1. The group may appear to listen and even agree, yet because they haven't been a part of the process, when the meeting is over they go back to work, and the ideas from the meeting don't stick. And they aren't implemented.

2. If there is discussion, you, the teller, waste time trying to convince people that your idea is the best. In that environment you lose neutrality. And you lose the benefit of your team's expertise. You don't ask for it when you're in telling mode, and therefore they don't give it.

3. In telling mode, you receive no honest feedback. Your communication style and cues, verbal and nonverbal, indicate you're not looking for feedback. Being in telling mode means potentially losing a competitive business edge. How can you be competitive when you're not really in the loop about what's going on in your business and your team?

4. Your team never learns to be creative problem-solvers because they don't have to think. You're always *telling* them what to do and fixing their problem. Or you revert to number two, convincing them your ideas are best and implying their ideas are not.

5. The team's talent and experience are wasted. When these things are left untapped, morale often drops. Have you ever wondered, "Why is this team so quiet, unengaged, and lacking energy?" Hmmm.

6. Your people become sheep, waiting for you to tell them what to do. They comply. Show up. Hope that there will be donuts (at least they will get something for their time). *Baaa.* "We usually have donuts. Where are the donuts? Don't we get a donut?"

So, what kinds of questions do we ask?

The #1 Facilitator Superpower: Open- and Closed-Ended Questions

I'm sure you've heard of open- and closed-ended questions before. Even if you think you're familiar with how to use them, please stay with me here. These questions can change your life.

It's important to use these two types of questions from the very beginning of the prework process and throughout discussions in meetings and projects.

Becoming a master of these questions is critical for your success.

Human beings are creatures of habit, as we discussed earlier in this chapter. As facilitators and leaders, we may not be aware we're in a telling mode. This same situation applies to asking questions. We may feel we *do* ask questions. But the *kind* of questions we ask and *how* we ask them make all the difference in the results we achieve.

Let's start by dissecting the most commonly used question.

Closed-ended Questions

Our habit as humans is to ask closed-ended questions. These are the questions that are answered with a yes or a no. Closed-ended questions have a role: they are decision-making questions. Your instruction to the brain is to make a decision. You're signaling two potential responses: agree or disagree, yes or no. As the name suggests, closed-ended questions *close* down conversation.

Closed-ended questions you commonly hear in meetings:

- Anything else?
- Anyone have ideas about this?
- Anybody have problems with this?
- Anything missing here?
- So we're all in agreement, right?
- Would you like to move in this direction?
- Would you like to talk about this?
- Do you want to talk about anything else?

- Are we done? Ready to move on?

If you've ever wondered, "Why doesn't anybody want to discuss this issue?" or, "This team doesn't talk much. Why are they so quiet?" you may want to listen closely to the questions you're asking. The team's behavior may be a symptom of your asking closed-ended questions. These questions close down creativity, because you're not *asking* the brain to be creative, you're asking it to make a decision.

"Is there anything else we need to talk about?"

"No."

(Because getting out of that meeting sooner rather than later is more important. And it's funny how we get exactly what we ask for.)

But wait! Closed-ended questions have an important role in a discussion. By all means, use closed-ended questions when your discussion is complete and it's time move forward. When the team is ready to make a decision, what's the action plan? This or that? However, if you want to stimulate creativity, engagement, conversation, and input? Use open-ended questions.

Start Discussions With the Secret Superpower

Open ended questions can't be answered with a yes or a no. Open-ended questions open up conversation and creativity and hook the mind. They require participant to think about their experiences, reflect on what they know, formulate opinions, and express feelings. Open-ended questions direct participants into the file cabinets in their brains where creativity, imagination, and innovative information are stored. There is no decision to be made. Not yet.

When open-ended questions are asked, control and participation in the conversation are passed to the participants. You'll get a completely different kind of conversation and participation level by asking open-ended questions. It's almost too simple. Deceptively simple.

The Art of Asking Open-Ended Questions

Here's the secret. Start your question with one of the following words: *what, how,* or *why*. It will be automatically open-ended. How cool is that? It's easy to remember and practice.

> *What.*
> *How.*
> *Why.*

If you think changing your team, increasing communication, and ramping up participation and creativity has to be more complex than this, you're not alone. People don't want to buy the fact that this small adjustment to how you ask questions can make such a big difference. Good news: it's true! This is a simple and powerful tool. You can start using it right away—you don't even have to download an app. And it will immediately change the quality of your meetings for the better. Check this out.

Here's a quick comparison.

Closed-ended question: "Any challenges here?"

"No."

Open-ended question: "What do you see as some of our biggest challenges?"

"Well, let me think..."

And then the ideas start to flow.

When you keep the open-ended questions active and alive, the team does the work.

> *We're making a great list here. What else are you seeing?*
> *Why do you think we did it that way?*
> *How is this impacting the team?*
> *What are the risks of going down this path?*

When the facilitator/leader asks open-ended questions, even at weekly department meetings, the team understands so much more about why they decided what they decided, the map that got them to where they decided to be, and how they're going to implement the decision—because they're the ones who thought it through, examined all options, recommended a course of action, and/or came up with the solution. Let loose the brilliance of your team. Let them do the work! Ask open-ended questions.

Resistance to Open-Ended Questions

Some people resist using open-ended questions. The excuse they use? "Closed-ended questions are faster." On the surface, that's true. They may end the meeting—and the discussion—faster. But a fast meeting isn't necessarily a great meeting. How do you measure success? It could be the opposite.

I've heard stressed out, tired, overworked team leaders say, "I don't have time to hear everyone's thoughts on this." Sometimes that is absolutely the case. A quick decision needs to be made. The team lead just wants to run something by his or her team as a quick check-in and ask, "Are we missing something here?"

Ask yourself: "Why am I getting these people together in this room for an hour or more? Why am I pulling them away from their desks and what they are working on? Could I get this information from them without pulling them into a meeting?"

If you want fast, and want to ask only closed-ended questions, consider alternatives. Could this be handled with an email? Or a quick teleconference?

It's a question of HABIT.

It's easy for closed-ended questions to become the default mode. It's a slippery slope.

As creatures of habit we revert to our home base, and for a lot of us that's the closed-ended question.

Where is your current home base?

1. Begin to listen, to yourself and to conversations going on

around you. How are questions posed? If they're answered
with a yes or a no, they're closed-ended questions.

2. Make it a game—the brain loves that. Change the closed-
ended questions you hear into open-ended ones using the
three magic words: **what, how,** and **why.**

3. As your radar becomes more finely tuned to open- and
closed-ended questions happening in conversations, your
own self-awareness will increase. When you hear yourself
beginning to ask a closed-ended question, change it up to an
open-ended one. "Anything else?" "Are we done?" These
closed-ended questions are so common we don't realize
we're asking them.

When you hear *any* or *are* coming out of your mouth, that's your
cue. Your lips are open, but before you start to say the words, make
the *w* sound like you're blowing out a candle (are you doing it right
now? Great!) and get that magic word inserted instead.

"Anything...." Oops! Reshape your lips, and say, *"What* else do we
want to talk about?"

If "Anything else?" slips right out, no worries—you can make the
save and insert the open-ended version right in behind it.

"Anything else? What else do we want to discuss?"

The good news is that no one will even know you're practicing.
And there's more good news. Everyday there are unending opportunities to practice mastering this critical facilitator superpower. Practice
at home. I've heard many life-changing stories about the results at
home and at work.

1. Turn up your radar and begin listening for open- and closed-
ended questions in conversations going on around you: at
the store, in the restaurant, on TV and webcasts, and
at home.

2. When you hear a closed-ended question, make it open using
what, how, or why.

3. Whenever possible, focus on using open-ended questions in conversation.

Kristine was a participant in our two-day *Super Meetings: Facilitation and Leadership Intensive*. The homework assignment at the end of day one was exactly what you were just assigned.

The next morning, we began with an interactive "walk the walls" day-one review. We literally walked around the room, observing and discussing the sticky notes and charts to get our brains warmed up and back to where we left off the day before. Next, we discussed the homework assignment.

What was your experience with the homework everybody? How'd it go?

Kristine immediately raised her hand. She was a department lead on a nuclear engineering project for an aircraft carrier. Smart, reserved, and well-groomed, she'd been fairly quiet on day one of the training session.

"I went home after the training last night and started to do the same thing I always do—grab a glass of wine, open up my home computer, and plop down on the couch. My husband Matt was already in his chair doing just that.

"We have a lovely deck and a pretty view. Sunset was coming on, and I thought, 'Geez, let me give this homework a try.'

"I said, 'Hey Matt, how about you join me out on the deck?'

"He immediately said, 'What's wrong?'

"I said 'Nothing. It's so pretty out, let's enjoy the view and talk.'"

Kristine shared that Matt needed a bit more convincing, certain that something was "wrong". The class chuckled, as did Kristine, yet there was something else being acknowledged.

"It was sad and a bit of a shock to see the routine we were in, without really realizing it. That an invitation to sit on our beautiful deck and talk meant something was *wrong*.

"I moved out to the deck with my wine, while repeating '*What, how, why*' in my mind. I'd set this up, and I was going to see it through. Matt suspiciously followed."

"'How was your day?'"

"Fine."

"What were you working on?"

"The Ersching Project."

"How is it going?"

"It's alright. We keep hitting this roadblock."

"How do you think you can get around it?"

"You know, I don't know Kristine. It really keeps me awake at night."

"Oh, I'm so sorry Matt. I didn't know that. How can I help?"

"Several hours later, in the dark, under the stars and into the next bottle of wine, we were laughing and telling stories, it was so fun. We both said, 'Oh my gosh, we haven't talked like this in a *long* time.' We went to bed." Then she paused and grinned. "And that's all I'm going to say about that!"

The class erupted in clapping and laughter. Priceless!

Later in the morning, the break was ending, the music stopped, and everyone was back in their seats. Kristine raised her hand.

Yes, what's up Kristine?

"I wanted to take a minute and follow up on the homework assignment.

"I got a voicemail from Matt. He's booked us a place at the beach for the weekend. We've been talking about doing this for a couple of years.

"I am SO grateful for the home work. Thank you, this stuff really works!"

Check it out for yourself. Let me know what you find. This one tool can change your life.

We circled back to the prework. Be careful what you're asking for. Know your session objective. Then you can ask the appropriate questions to get the information you need and achieve the objective you've set.

Asking versus telling requires a mindset shift. What kind of leader are you? What kind of leader do you want to be? People can quickly discern if you're behaving authentically, and whether your words, actions, and intentions match. Who will you *be* for this team? As a mentor of mine says, "Does your audio match your video?"

Practice

Let's use this question to practice: "Does your audio match your video?"

What kind of question is it? Open? Closed?

How is it answered?

With a yes or a no, right? That means it's closed.

Great job! Give yourself a high five!

When to Use Open, When to Use Closed

When you ask open-ended questions, you get increased participation, deeper and richer discussions, and more opinions, ideas, and solutions. This kind of discussion will take more time.

A discussion to generate ideas or solve problems or plan actions will be best served with an abundance of open-ended questions. If you're under pressure to make a quick decision, closed-ended may be the best option.

Think of asking open and closed ended questions like eating an ice cream cone.

Imagine your favorite kind of ice cream—all the creamy goodness, the tastes, textures, sensations, smells and feelings, as your mouth dives into those exquisite first bites. The rich thick yellowy vanilla, the gooey, salty caramel swirling and tangling up with the dark-chocolate-covered almond bits...

Those are the kinds of details we want to tap into by asking open ended questions.

- What does it look like?
- What does it sound like, feel like, even smell like?
- What are we looking to make happen here?
- Why? What would be the benefit of that?

- How does it look when it's working?
- Why does it happen the way it does now?
- How can we adjust it?
- What are some tweaks to make it work even better?

After generating a deliciously thorough list—you've eaten all of your ice cream—and you've gathered all the details, you will likely experience a lull.

You have arrived at the crunchy cone. Conversation slows. The list is full, not much left to say. That's your cue to begin *closing* the discussion by using closed-ended questions.

> *Great list. Is there anything we've missed? Anything else?*

Heads shake. No, nothing.

> *Are we ready to move forward? Turn to your neighbor and say,*
> *"Great job on that!" Give them a fist bump!*

On to the next agenda item. BAM! Just like that.

Changing Closed-Ended Questions to Open-Ended Questions

CLOSED	OPEN
Anything else?	What else?
Anyone have ideas about this??	What else do you see here? What ideas come to mind? What could we do?
Anybody have problems with this?	What problems do you see?
Would you like to talk about this?	What do we need to talk about here?
Do you want to talk about anything else?	What's left to discuss?
Are we done?	How close are we to completing this?
Anything missing here?	What's missing here?
So we're all in agreement, right?	How are you feeling about where we're at? How close to agreement are we? What's left to discuss so we can agree?
Would you like to move in this direction?	What are the benefits of moving in this direction? Let's take a look at this. Why would we choose to move in this direction?

Laser-Focused Listening

Now that you're generating exceptional discussions with your masterful open-ended questions, the next leadership muscle to exercise is your capacity for laser-focused listening.

Listening is a skill that can be learned and practiced. Listening is also a choice. The next time you find yourself in a conversation, resist the urge to speak or to comment. Notice what your mind is doing while someone else is talking. Often, we're already thinking about what we're going to say back and forming our response. Often, we're having our own conversation, in our heads, about what we're hearing, and either agreeing or disagreeing. Or, we're not listening at all; instead, we've tuned out and are making the grocery list.

Practice listening without interrupting. Wait until the speaker is finished with his or her idea. Notice the minds tendency to wander and let other thoughts take over. When you notice this, bring yourself back to the conversation. Stay laser focused on what that person is saying in the moment. This will build your listening muscles. You will also become more discerning about what you ask for.

Decide to listen. Choose to focus like a laser on what the speaker is saying, as if what you're hearing will change your life! This is an act of respect for your team. Bring them your best. Be the model of exceptional leadership and facilitation.

EIGHTEEN

Managing Time

---

*H*ow you do anything is how you do everything.

How you show up in the little things is how you'll show up in the big things.

I've been training teams for more than two decades, and I often ask, "What drives you crazy about meetings? What are the things that make you want to scream 'Get me outta here'?"

One of the first things I hear, 99.9 per cent of the time, is this: "Meetings that start and end late!"

Watch out for the unspoken messages you're sending. It looks really lame if you can't get a meeting started on time. Every minute you wait, people get increasingly agitated. *Starting* the session late is starting the session off track. It's not a good way to begin.

If the leader supports holding up the start of a meeting for late arrivers, then he or she is part of the problem.

I've seen leaders repeatedly start meetings late, saying, "Hey, I really want to be respectful of your time, but let's give the late arrivers as few more minutes."

If you have ever been tempted to say this, or you have said this in the past, consider just how ridiculous this is. Because what I heard is you *want* to be respectful of your team's time, *but* you're *not* going to be. In fact, you're going to make everyone who got there on time—the behavior you want—wait for those who are late. You're rewarding the behavior you *don't* want.

The leader is setting the bar for expectations very low, perhaps unconsciously. The unspoken message is this: it's okay to be late. We'll even wait.

From the facilitator's perspective, this seems to be about the team and their ability to get to the meeting on time. From the team's perspective, it's a mushy-gray mixed message from the facilitator about start time. "When will the meeting *really* start? Maybe I can get a few more minutes of productive work done at my desk instead of sitting and waiting for you to decide when you'll start the meeting— because everyone knows your reputation for starting late. Just sayin'."

Why do we allow this? What keeps this in place when we know it's disrespectful and it drives people crazy?

The meeting invite says start time is 10:00 a.m. Whether it starts five, seven, or ten minutes late doesn't matter. The first face-to-face opportunity to demonstrate to your team where you set the bar for performance, efficiency, and respect for people's time has just been wasted.

The people who did arrive on time take note. Some don't react because starting late is such an ingrained habit. Others utter a resigned sigh. "Here we go again." Others may experience full-on frustration. "When is this thing going to get started? I've got a deadline today. I don't have time to be sitting here waiting for people who can't get it together to be on time. Everyone needs to get their act together."

This is the first crack in your credibility.

Building trust can take a long time. Destroying trust takes only seconds. An accumulation of lots of little things create your reputation and impact your organization.

Many leaders actually train people that it's okay to be late. They punish the people who found a way to get there on time and are modeling the behavior they want, by making them sit there and wait for the meeting to start. They reward the dysfunctional behavior by waiting for the late-comers, and then waste more time bringing them up to speed. Late people are honored! If the meeting has started without them, there is some unwritten idea that the meeting must stop when they arrive, and everyone is expected to catch them up. Most teams don't know how to address this habit or change it, so it continues.

On Time Every Time

When you start a meeting on time, you build on the trust and respect you began to cultivate in your prework. It means your actions and your words are congruent. (Your audio matches your video.) Starting on time showcases your ability to be punctual, gracefully corraling your team, following the agreements that were emailed out, and honoring those who are exhibiting the behavior you're looking for on your team.

The right little things done well can build a strong team, just as the wrong little things can wear down and tear down a team.

I was leading a two-day facilitation training session. The building was a new modern tower. Sheathed in glass, it seemed a perfect fit for this young, hip team. When I got off the elevator and arrived at the reception desk, I saw that the whole floor was walled in plexiglass. We were on the seventeenth floor, and the view was stunning.

Like so many other offices, this one had cubicles. These, though, were also plexiglass. You could see into everyone's cubes, into the hallway, and outside. Their central room was the conference room, where the training would be held.

I was forty-five minutes early. I walked into the conference room and started to set up. I hung the charts, set the manuals out, tested the sound system and teed up my music. It was getting closer and closer to start time. I could see people in their offices. One guy had his feet up on his desk doing something on his computer. Some were talking on the phone, a couple of small groups chatted as they tucked in to get their day started. They could also see me setting up. I saw a few faces peeking over their computers to see what was happening in the conference room, presumably checking whether anyone else was there and whether they should go.

The welcome email had gone out one month before the training and again two weeks later. Everyone knew the meeting was slated to start at nine. When my timer went off for the two-minute warning, I was still the only one in the room. Two minutes later, I was still the only one in the room. It was the first time (and only time, so far) this had happened to me. What to do? Go out and call to them like a mother hen? That didn't feel quite right, nor would it be the behavior I look to instill in a team. So I started the meeting. On time. All alone, in a conference room walled in plexiglass.

"How many of you have ever thought your work flow process could be even better?" I raised my hand.

As I continued through the opening-the-session script, I looked out at the employees, more of whom were now looking at me. I could see somebody hang up the phone, someone else grabbing her bag and a sweater, someone filling his water bottle at the fountain. They began moving toward the training room with looks on their faces that ranged from curious to confused.

Someone said, "I didn't know you were going to start right on the time!"

I said, "Oh, yes. On time. Every time."

They didn't know what to think. (I didn't either!)

These people were experts in their field. I knew they were smart and quick on the technical side of their business. Remember that meetings are like a petri dish of your organization: what's happening on a micro level can be an indicator of what's affecting the organization on a macro level. This team's people-side issues were impacting the technical side of their business.

One of the first steps in opening the session (we'll talk more about opening the session in Section VI: Mechanics of a Great Meeting) is to get the participants to confirm their objectives for the course. I ask what drives them crazy in meetings, and what they want to know when they walk out of the training. One of this team's biggest complaints was, "Our meetings never start on time!" Hmmm.

For the rest of the session, no one showed up late after breaks, after lunch, or the next day. I didn't need to remind them. I did say, "Thanks so much for getting back from break on time. This really helps us stay right on track!"

This experience is consistent for me across all meetings I facilitate: once I've set the tone, the performance bar, and the expectations around starting and ending on time, teams respond. They like it.

When expectations are clearly communicated and modeled, people know where the bar is set—and their performance improves to hit or exceed the bar.

At the end of the second day when we were closing the session and going over their objectives to make sure we had covered everything, we all had a good chuckle about how I started the meeting on time even though no one was in the room. The team made a great observation about their own blind spots regarding habits of showing up late; it had become a habit because there were no consequences for doing so. This led to a larger conversation about other blind spots that might exist in their organization. "If we don't hold ourselves accountable to show up on time, how else might this show up in how we do our work?" Fascinating, juicy stuff.

The secret to starting the meeting on time is really simple.

Start the meeting on time!

When the CEO or Leader Doesn't Show Up on Time

I was working with a leadership team that had received a prework welcome letter outlining the five pillars and the meeting logistics, including the exact start time and location. Our start time was 8:00 a.m. At 7:50 a.m., the CEO of the firm was still not there. The CEO's number two person, came up to tell me we wouldn't start until Mary, the CEO, was in the room.

"Geez," I said. "I don't want to keep everyone who *is* here on time waiting. In the prework, we discussed starting on time and I believe Mary is on board with that. I will take full responsibility."

His face twisted. He looked horrified. Shaking his head, he walked away. When I gave the two-minute warning—"Hey everyone, we'll be starting in two minutes. Now is a good time to get something to drink, get tucked in, and power down electronics. Thanks!"—the CEO was still not in the room, and her number two was rubbing his temples with his forefingers. He was throwing an Oscar-worthy stink face my way.

I started the meeting on time. Mary arrived, about ten minutes late. She came up to me at the first break and said, "I am so sorry. I was on a call, and I couldn't get here. Glad you didn't keep my team waiting. Thank you for starting on time." And she never showed up late again during our two and a half days together.

Starting before a key person shows up is a big concern in some teams? Why?

I think it's a habit, based on good intentions, protocol, or a misconception about manners and showing respect to the leader. The problem is that dysfunction starts to bubble up. The leader, who is exhibiting dysfunctional behavior, is rewarded. This person suffers no consequences for arriving late. The leader is also, perhaps unconsciously, setting the bar for the team's performance.

When a leader arrives late, it's disrespectful to all who are kept waiting. Layer on this apology I've heard a number of times: "Sorry I'm late. I don't want to be disrespectful of your time."

I always look around the room and see people rolling their eyes, shifting in their seats. The late leader is unaware of how his or her say-one-thing-and-do-another behavior is landing in the room. Audio not matching video.

What happens when the leader sets the don't-start-without-me expectation?

1. The leader who doesn't like it if they arrive to find a meeting has started without them wants the discussion to stop and for others to bring them up to speed on what they missed.

When this happens consistently, it is dysfunctional behavior that is condoned by the organization.

2. This behavior can be tied to the leader's emotional intelligence (EQ). There are leaders who have been promoted into their leadership role because they are great on the technical side of their job. In many of these cases, unfortunately, their EQ has not been as well-developed as their technical skills. They can consciously or unconsciously use their authority as a leader to control and manipulate their teams. The focus is on them, rather than on how their behavior impacts the team and their work. They behave more like a dictator than a caring leader. Their empathy and self-awareness are low. They show up to the meeting late, everyone waits, and there are no apologies.

Consider this approach. When you know solid prework has been completed with the team and the leader, start on time. If the leader arrives late and asks, "You started without me? What did I miss? Who will catch me up?" be ready for the room to go silent and for everyone to be look at you.

If the leader just missed the first fifteen to twenty minutes, here's your script:

> *No worries, we're just getting started. We're covering the welcome and overview. Here's your seat.*

Pick up where you left off. Own the room. Check in with the leader at break.

If they are more than thirty minutes late and you're into the data, here's your script:

> *Understood. And* (not but) *we're heading into a break shortly. Who here will bring* (name) *up to speed at break? Thanks. We're talking about* (topic) *and Jared was saying ... Jared, finish that thought. Thanks!*

Ninety percent of the time I've had great success with that strategy.

The other ten percent? The boss says, "Uh, no, that's *not* okay with me. I'd like to be brought up to speed right now."

In those push back cases, it's not worth a power struggle. Bring them up to speed.

Use your facilitator super powers for good.

> *Okay team, let's press 'pause.' Great discussion. Let's bring (name) up to speed. Take a moment and think back to the beginning of our session. We began with the welcome and opening. What did we talk about first? Where did we begin?*

Use this rewind as an opportunity for the team to review their work so far. Get them involved by asking open-ended questions and get the boss up to speed.

The Other Side of Starting Late = Ending Late

One thing we know for sure about meetings is that even your well-planned, prework-completed meeting can run longer than expected. Discoveries will be made as the team analyzes data, and, a proposed solution to a problem may require research before a decision about its feasibility can be made. Plan for the unplanned.

As soon as you find your projected timing is off and you're not going to be able to complete all the agenda items, or you're getting behind on timing and it looks like the meeting will run over, let the team know. Don't pretend you don't see this coming, and don't ignore the fact that the meeting time is running over.

> *Hey everybody, I know we decided to discuss this…*

Or:

> *Since we'll need to break to gather more info…*

Or:

> *It looks like we won't have enough time to complete this last agenda item and still finish on time. How would you like to handle this?*
>
> *Let's look at the agenda. What do we need to complete here today? What can wait? Or, what if the meeting runs longer than expected?*
>
> *I imagine we could wrap up everything if we stayed for thirty more minutes. Who would be able to do that? Who would not? Could we complete the agenda with a partial team?*

Let the team decide.

If the meeting is supposed to finish at 4:00, by 4:01 you're already losing them. Don't hold your team hostage. Their brains are asking, "How long is this going to go on? How long will I have to sit here? This is *so* rude!" It erodes trust and respect and your reputation as a leader.

Running late is the worst-case scenario. If you get done early, that's the best-case scenario, right? Everybody is cheering, "Yeah! We got done early!" Any time there's a shift off the planned agenda, let them know what you see and what the costs, both positive and negative, of diverting from the plan will be.

Use open-ended questions. Let's say the team says, "Even though it's not on the agenda, we really, really need to talk about this."

> *Okay. What do you want to see happen at the end of this discussion? What's the mini-objective of this discussion? What will it get us? Because we're going to veer off our agenda here.*

"Well, we'll get this, this, and this."

> *Okay. How does that sound to everybody? Is that worth it to us?*

And then they say, "Yes, that's the way we want to go."

> *Okay. What are the cons going to be? We may not get this other*
> *stuff done. How many of you can live with that for today?*
> *Okay, good. What else do we need to do in the meantime?*

It's all open-ended questions. *You* don't figure it out; you let the team become the problem-solvers, the strategists. If the meeting is supposed to end at 4:30, don't wait until 4:15, or even worse, wait until 4:30, to say, *I want to be respectful of your time, and we're just going to have to run over a little bit.* It's not respectful to ask participants to stay longer than they'd planned, especially when you've given them no advance notice.

A rule of thumb is to alert the team of the potential to run late an hour in advance in a half-day session, and twenty minutes in advance in an hour-long session.

As facilitator, creating boundaries and staying on track are your responsibilities. Being brave and not rewarding dysfunctional behavior is part of the territory you travel to execute those responsibilities. You become the model of exceptional leadership in action.

The skillful management of time is a facilitator superpower. Work your magic.

NINETEEN

Energy

---

*E*nergy is a key facilitator superpower. Let's look at the science behind this success tool.

In her TED talk, *My Stroke of Insight*, Dr. Jill Bolte Taylor describes her experience of having a stroke at age thirty-seven. As a neuroscientist who studies the brain, she observed her stroke as a clinician while simultaneously experiencing its effects personally and physically.

Dr. Bolte Taylor teaches that there are two distinct halves of the brain. The right brain helps us focus on the here and now. It thinks in pictures. It transforms information about the present moment into an energy stream that is directed to all our sensory systems: how it looks, smells, tastes, sounds, and feels. It sees connections between everyone and everything.

The left brain is quite different. It is home to everything linear and methodical, to the past and present. The left brain picks out elements of the present moment, organizes and categorizes them, and associates them with everything we've ever learned or experienced in our past. Then, it projects that onto the future. It thinks in words, connects our internal and external worlds, and sees us as distinct and apart from all else.

When Dr. Bolte-Taylor experienced a stroke in the left side of her brain, she lost language, the ability to move, and her past and future.

Imagine: no baggage, no trauma, no to-do list, no stress. She describes this as nirvana.

The stroke didn't affect her right brain, which continued to bring in data on the environment around her. As she lay in her hospital bed, it became clear that what she could perceive, without the distraction of the left brain, was the energy people brought with them into her room, how they were *being*, and how this impacted her healing, positively and negatively.

When nurses and doctors made eye contact, smiled, talked to her, touched her with care, and explained what they were going to do, she felt better. When she was ignored, or moved and poked without a greeting or acknowledgment, she felt depleted. Although the tests and procedures being done were exactly the same, *how* they were being done made all the difference.

As she recuperated, Jill continued to experience the very real impact of her caretakers' energy influencing her recovery and healing. Her mantra became:

"Please be responsible for the energy you bring into my room."

During a recent session on energy and leadership, we were discussing how standing up when leading a meeting raises the energy level of the entire team. The group was engaged and curious while clarifying why standing up—which appears simple—is so important. A fun exchange of ideas was happening.

Then Carla, a department head in her early fifties, quiet, legs crossed, arms crossed, and face tight, spoke up. Her voice was strained. "*I'm* a systems analyst. Because I *have* to type the minutes *and* take notes—nobody else will do it—I *sit* during our meetings. I'm *old* and my back *hurts*. I don't *like* to get up in front of people. I don't think I should have to stand."

I watched people's faces cringe and bodies flinch as Carla spoke. The happy little trolley of our discussion that was chugging right along collided with Clara's energy and went right off the rails.

Maybe you've seen a discussion derailed in this way in your meetings—words and how they were said sucked the energy right out of the room.

When you're the facilitator and leader, the kind of energy you bring into the room is constantly on display. Let's look at this idea of energy in two different kinds of meetings.

Meeting #1

You walk into the meeting room. The leader, mumbling under their breath, is trying to log on to the computer to get their PowerPoint loaded. A person sitting toward the back is hunched over, texting. In a corner, another attendee is typing on their computer. Other than the light tapping of the keyboards, there's silence.

More attendees arrive. Some sit at the conference table, some take seats around the perimeter of the room. A couple of small groups begin chatting. The leader is still trying to log on. Several people arrive a few minutes past 8:00 a.m., which was to be the start time.

The leader finally has the PowerPoint loaded, and says "Where's Jim?" (Jim is the department head.) "Let's give him a few more minutes."

Some of the people who made it to the meeting on time continue talking and working, and a few leave to get a cup of coffee in the break room. Jim arrives at 8:07. The meeting leader says, "Okay. Let's get started."

The blinds are closed, the lights are turned off, and the PowerPoint presentation begins. The coffee-getters return. The next thirty minutes are spent describing last quarter's trends. Tiny bell curves and intersecting pie charts with unreadable words present the resuts. There are a couple questions from the team about numbers and what they might mean. The technical questions are answered. And the slides continue. As does the texting, whispering, and eye rolling. A team member's eyes close, his head bobs forward, and then a sharp snap back up. Ouch. Chuckles can be heard. None of this dysfunction is addressed by the leader, who is focused on the screen rather than the team.

A teammate asks, "So what do you want us to do with this data?"

"Well, I thought you should see this," says the leader. "Any questions?" Heads shake no. "Uh, okay. Guess we're done. Remember, end of quarter reports are due Friday."

Mumbling is heard as people file out. *Baaaa, baaaa, baaaa.* And no donuts!

OMG! Poke me in the eye. Really?

Please revisit Section I: Leadership Fundamentals, where we discussed the negative impacts of bad meetings, in particular the costs of meeting like this one in salaries alone. Add the intangible costs. Expensive, right? Especially for poor results.

Meeting #2

You leave your desk ten minutes early for a two-hour meeting, which is supposed to start at 8:00 a.m. The meeting invite, more of a welcome email really, promised a prompt start. We'll see.

As you get closer to the conference room you hear The Beatles song, "Here Comes the Sun" playing. You enter the room and see five charts on the front wall.

Session Objective
- *Develop action plan for Q4.*

Agenda
- *Welcome and overview*
- *Q3 results*
- *What is this telling us?*
- *Course corrections?*
- *Action plan*
- *Review & close*

Agreements
- *Respect the speaker*
- *All ideas welcome*
- *Freedom to disagree*
- *Start and end on time*

• *All electronics off*

Consensus Decision Making
• *I can live with this decision/idea and support it*
• *Consensus doesn't mean: I think this is the best or only solution.*

Parking Lot
(This sheet will be blank until the meeting gets going.)

As you scan the five charts, you recall that this information was in the email you received about this meeting.

The meeting leader greets you with a smile and a handshake. "Hey, thanks so much for being early. Grab a cup of coffee. I just made us a fresh pot. I also made name tents. We'll be working in teams. See yours over there? You're on the blue team! Oh, do you know Sam? He's on the blue team too. Hey Sam, this is Tim."

The music continues in the background. The facilitator greets people as they arrive. Two minutes before the meeting is scheduled to start you hear the facilitator say, "Hey everybody, this is your two minute warning. We'll be starting in two minutes. Now is a great time power down electronics, grab a drink, and take care of last-minute business. Thanks!"

You and the other attendees begin to sit down and get tucked in. Several members haven't arrived yet. *Beep, beep, beep—* the timer goes off. The facilitator begins. He projects his voice, grabbing your attention. It's like an invisible rope corralling everybody into their seats. His smile and enthusiasm are both unusual and refreshing .

Right away, he outlines the five charts on the wall: session objective, agenda, agreements, decision-making, and parking lot. A few more team members trickle in and find their seats. Everyone is now seated together at the U-shaped table.

After he gives a ten-minute overview of Q3 results using a bulleted poster on the wall, the discussion begins in small groups, giving everyone a chance to participate. "Thinking back on the last three months, what's working? What's been challenging? What are the Q3 results telling us?" Animated discussion continues. After fifteen minutes, the small groups come back together into the large team to share their ideas. People are engaged, and participation is high. Improving communication is identified as a key driver to increasing performance and employee satisfaction.

The team agrees on a first approach to improve the communication loop—from the field to leadership and leadership back to the field. A sub-team is formed and already has an easy win chosen with the agreement of the team.

The facilitator says, "Great job team! Give your neighbors a high five!"

High fives and smiles are shared around the table. The meeting ends on time. And without a PowerPoint in sight.

Meeting #1 or Meeting #2?

Which meeting would you rather attend? What's one of the key differences between these two meetings?

Energy. In Meeting #2, the facilitator's energy is upbeat, positive, and contagious.

When you're the facilitator, the team will model your energy. In my experience, people in a group will set their energy level to 50 to 75 percent of the leader's energy.

I've heard concerns from leaders about ramping up their energy for meetings. The idea of increasing the volume of their voice, looking and acting enthused and interested generates fear. They're afraid they will look stupid or weird. They worry about what people will think of them. Will they be judged as a flake, or unprofessional, or crazy? They tell me "I'm an introvert."

Hey, I get it.

Doing something new and different requires a period of learning and practice to help you transition from uncomfortable to comfortable. And what I'm suggesting requires you to practice in front of a group of your teammates—live.

Standing up in front of a room of people, people who may have issues with the meeting objective, people who may be your boss, or your boss's boss, is not for the faint of heart.

The left hemisphere of the brain says, "No, not a good idea. Based on the files I have stored for you, you don't have a lot of experience or training in this area. This looks like a potential threat. Back away." Bless your heart, left hemisphere. But you've got this.

There are two things to keep in mind.

First, energy is a *skill* related to the people side of business. It's an essential component of leadership, and yet one of the least taught. When is the last time you received training on energizing yourself and modeling inspiration, motivation, trust, and resilience?

And second, energy is a *tool*. It can be learned and practiced. Energy requires preparation. Doing the prework begins this process. When we are prepared, our confidence increases. That impacts how we show up.

When we aren't prepared and we stand in a front of a team without proper training and skills, without a solid agenda let alone an objective, without agreements for behavior, and without knowing how to start on time or keep the team on track, dysfunction rises up. We spend our energy focusing on the fallout we've created by being unprepared.

No wonder people have uncomfortable experiences facilitating. We are hesitant to be vulnerable because we don't want to look stupid and unprofessional in front of the group. So, we often hold back, stay small, hoping to get through the meeting under the radar. We let the PowerPoint lead the meeting and use it as a crutch for the skills we were never trained to have.

If you walk in the meeting pinging off the wall—rah rah rah—yes, you'll look crazy. That's not what I'm talking about. That's not authentic.

What I am talking about is this scenario: You've done prework; you know the session objective and the agenda. You have practiced and are comfortable with asking open-ended and closed-ended questions. You've even written some down on your notes as cues just in case you need them. You've rehearsed the opening-the-session script (we'll get to this in more detail in Section VI, Mechanics of a Great Meeting) so you can provide an overview and kick off the meeting with confidence. You have a plan for each agenda item: a small group discussion, large group debrief, team exercise, etc. And, you start and the end meeting on time.

Do this with confidence and a smile on your face, with the attitude of service and caring, and I guarantee you will change your meetings and your teams. When you get comfortable up front facilitating, you become more relaxed. The energy in the room changes. In a relaxed environment, the team can tap into their right brain where creativity and imagination live, where ideas and solutions are richer and more expansive. Out-of-the-box ideas spark new approaches to long standing challenges. (This stuff really happens. I've seen it countless times.) Now add more training and practice, and a little music. This is the recipe I've used to coach facilitators who have gone on to quickly transform their teams from sluggish to super. Teams *want* to be engaged and perform at a high level. Give them permission to be awesome by your example.

Beware of the left brain working overtime to keep us in our comfort zone.

What I hear just below the surface of many comments on ramping up your energy is resistance. Resistance to change. We humans are creatures of habit. On the technical side of business, we're constantly asked to change: computer-system updates, process improvements, new product lines. I'm suggesting we also need to demand, expect, and be more open to change on the *people* side of business. And a lot of the work we do—or don't get done—happens with people in the context of a meeting.

Updating and improving the processes on the people side of our business is critical to our overall success. The ability to calibrate and use energy as a tool in meetings can be learned and practiced.

Easy Ways to Increase Your Energy

Begin to notice the left brain's habit of thinking about what others might be thinking about you. Switch that thinking up. Instead, focus your attention on how you can serve the team.

What do they need? How can I support them? Ask yourself these open-ended questions to find out.

Take a quiet moment. Toggle over to your right brain and imagine yourself as the world's greatest facilitator and leader. How are you showing up? How are you walking, talking? What are you wearing? What are you saying and doing? Write this down.

Now pick one or two of the following ideas and test them out.

- Treat yourself as a precious object. If you don't, who will?
- Eat healthy food. Drink lots of water.
- Practice smiling. This is a great power and energy tool. (Remember that 50 to 75 percent of what you model gets adopted by your team.)
- Say thank you.
- Look people in the eye.
- Listen. All the way until they're done talking.
- Infuse some fun into the work you're doing.
- Buy your team lunch. Or bake cookies for them. Doing nice things for others has a two-fold effect: others feel good and you do too.

Facilitating With Energy: Your Big Voice

Remember that your voice is an important tool in managing the group and keeping the session on track. While you're facilitating, set your volume one to two levels above a normal conversational voice. Imagine you're turning up the volume dial a couple of clicks on your radio. It might feel as though you're way too loud. You're not. People will fall asleep if they can't hear you. People will become distracted and do something else if they can't hear you. And, if people can't hear you, the meeting will be a big waste of everyone's time. If you talk in a normal conversational voice, you will lose the back half of the room.

Increasing your volume means using your diaphragm and lower belly. This isn't shouting or yelling. It's projecting. If the discussions become emotional or passionate and the participants get louder, you must get even louder than they're being to focus their attention.

Reset your volume, along with your energy, at the beginning of each agenda item, and when people are coming back from break. Write yourself a reminder note on your agenda to do this.

Beware of the Little Voice

What does your little voice (you know, that voice in your head that provides a running commentary throughout the day and then wakes you up in the night to have a meeting about your day, your week, your life) say to you about energy, projection, and volume when you're leading meetings?

Listen for this: "Don't be too loud—they'll think you're crazy, you'll look like a fool…" The little voice is a survival mechanism that wants to keep you in your comfort zone, the safe zone, where there is no danger. When you're up in front of a room, and you hear it start talking, lovingly say, "Thanks, I've got this. You can take a rest." Replace the little voice with a question: "What does the group need right now? How can I support them?"

If you want to be a great leader versus an okay one, *you do not have the luxury of being small.* Being up front will push every button you have. This can be an enormous gift. You will grow as a person, and as a leader, through your work facilitating meetings.

Energy Vacuums

Be aware of your own energy. Energy waxes and wanes depending on the time of day, your stress levels, how much sleep you've had, how much and what kind of food you've eaten and how hydrated you are. Pay attention, and manage your energy accordingly.

Make note of these lull times when you book your meeting:

Mid-morning: 10:30 — 11:00
After lunch: 1:00 — 2:00
Mid-afternoon: 3:00 — 3:30

During these energy vacuums and throughout the session make sure you're doing the following:

- Breaking the team into a small groups for activities
- Getting them up and moving around.
- Walking around the room and reviewing the posted charts. I call this "walking the walls."
- Leading the group in a stretch or follow the leader. (I know, Little Voice. Follow the leader sounds silly. Thanks for sharing!) This activity is a game-changer for even the most formal groups.
- Encouraging high fives or fist bumps after the completion of each agenda item, and having team members turn to their neighbors and say, "Great job." This helps you to build momentum.
- Getting them to stand up.
- Bringing out the toys (Nerf balls, Play-Doh).
- Thinking about ways to turn data into a training game (e.g., Bingo or Jeopardy); the brain likes to play.
- Taking breaks as needed, based on energy levels (this is a good reason not to post times on your agenda). Treats and healthy snacks can help energy stay high.

Avoid these activities during energy vacuums:

- Giving long, detailed PowerPoint presentations.
- Having people read documents and other technical materials.
- Turning down the lights for PowerPoint presentations or

videos.

Focus on Your Energy

Energy is the difference between good and great facilitation and between good and great leadership.

If you want your team members to be upbeat and optimistic hard workers with confidence in their ability to deal with the issues they're facing, exhibit these same qualities when you're in front of the group. You can only take your team as far as *you* are willing to go.

Your attitude, preparation, and intention all begin in the prework phase. Set your intention as you prepare for the meeting by asking yourself, "As the leader/facilitator, how can I serve this team? What kind of leader do I want to be?"

Be responsible for the energy you bring into any room. Energy is an attractive force. The energy you bring into the room will attract more of that energy.

People's dysfunction sometimes gets blamed when meetings or projects aren't going well. Often dysfunction is a symptom. The real root cause is that the meeting and their facilitation sucks. If you're not getting the results you would like on your team, do a facilitator check-in: "How is my energy and performance impacting my team?"

Be mindful of your own feelings about this meeting and/or project. How are you talking about it? What are you communicating to others by virtue of your tone, your expectations, and your energy? How will that impact the results?

Be the boss of your own brain. Don't let your brain boss you around. Begin observing the chatter in your head. What do you think about? What things are you saying to yourself? What do you say about others? How are these thoughts and ideas nourishing you? How might they be poison? You can push pause or delete on any of these conversations.

Facilitation and leadership are about service. They're about running interference, removing roadblocks, and guiding the team to the objective. Your job is to pick the right team and to know your company's objective, your project objective, your meeting objective. Do the prework and set your team up for success. Think about how your team would be affected if you set your intention, every day, to be the world's greatest facilitator and leader. What might happen if you believed the most important part of your job was to *be* the model of energy, optimism, resilience, kindness and trustworthiness?

Building your capacity to toggle from your right brain to left and back again allows you to gather the full spectrum of data available in the moment to artfully facilitate your team. Being aware of how you show up for your team, of the energy you bring and how that energy influences and impacts them and their work is a facilitator super power.

Use your superpowers for good!

TWENTY

Emotional Intelligence

*J*n our technology-driven world it's common to spend the majority of our time in the left hemisphere of the brain, sorting out details and categorizing information so we can make plans and take actions to achieve goals. This is the home of our IQ, or intelligence quotient.

The right side of the brain is the emotional, feeling side. It takes in information through the senses—sight, sound, touch, taste, and smell—and it processes our feelings. This side of the brain interprets people's facial expressions, tone of voice, and how they're behaving.

Our emotional intelligence, or EQ, is based on what we *do* with that information. How able are we to take these inputs, including our feelings, and decide whether and how to respond or react?

EQ is a leadership superpower. Developing our understanding of how our tone and behavior affects others is what emotional intelligence is all about.

In my experience, only 20 percent of projects and teams go off track because of the technical content. Eighty percent of them go off track because of the *people side* of what's happening in the room. It's *how* the discussion is happening and why. Leaders and facilitators with high EQ will positively affect the results and overall success of the team. Teams that fall apart are typically dysfunctional, low-performing, poor communicators, and poor collaborators. There's nothing wrong with their data. You've heard me say it before: it's the people side of the business that matters. Leading well requires fluency in emotional intelligence.

Staying Neutral

EQ is what allows you to manage your emotions and feelings. It's what helps you stay neutral even while facilitating discussions that trigger your opinions, values, and beliefs. It helps you stay calm when situations become volatile and emotionally charged. And it helps you take appropriate action quickly with a reactive group to prevent a dip in effectiveness and a spike in dysfunction. It will allow you to communicate clearly in a way that's inclusive, not condescending or dismissive, so nobody gets hurt. You'll use all the input available from both your right and left brain. If you find yourself getting angry or upset about what people are saying, pay attention to that. It's a signal to super-engage and dig deeper into your own EQ toolbox.

In your prework, as you talk to and pick your A-team, you will begin to get a sense of the EQ of individuals and the team in general. That's the great news about the tools and strategies we've been discussing so far: the prework, the five pillars, open-ended questions, and your energy all create a safety net for you as the leader and facilitator no matter the EQ of the participants in the room.

The Five Key Areas of Emotional Intelligence

American psychologist and author Daniel Goleman popularized the concepts of emotional intelligence and its impact and power, and broke it down into these five key areas.

Self-awareness = what do I know about myself?

Self-regulation = how do I handle myself?

Motivation = how do I energize myself?

Empathy = how well do I see others' perspectives and motivations and put myself in their shoes?

Social skills = what is my capacity to create, build and maintain relationships? (The focus is on others, not you.)

1. Self-awareness.

Self-awareness means recognizing emotions as they happen, understanding their root causes, and your triggers. Being able to evaluate and understand your emotions means you can begin to better manage them. Self-awareness is also accompanied by confidence in your worth and your competencies. As a facilitator, knowing what pushes your buttons will help you keep an even keel while steering the meeting ship. You will be able to *respond* rather than *react* when course corrections are needed. And you won't let others goad you into an inflammatory response.

2. Self-regulation.

We may not be able to control *when* we experience a particular emotion, but self-regulation means we can influence *how and when we express* that emotion. It also means managing impulsivity: when we can identify and name our emotions, we can disconnect the pipeline between our emotions and our behavior. And when we can change our behavior *in spite of* our emotions, because we understand how it affects others and impacts our relationships, well, that's EQ nirvana. People with high EQ are able to, in real time, process what they're about to say before they say it, and understand the consequences of their words. Their minds are a couple of steps ahead of what comes out of their mouths.

3. Motivation.

Clear goals and a positive attitude are pre-requisites for being able to motivate yourself and others. Even if you're not naturally disposed to optimism, you can learn to reframe negative thoughts into positive ones, which will help you inspire others and achieve your goals. Motivation requires a commitment to taking initiative and a consistent effort to improve.

How do you inspire and lift your team's spirits, especially during challenges?

How do you model resiliency and navigate unexpected events that would stop others?

4. Empathy.

Recognizing how other people are feeling is a key skill for any leader or facilitator of great meetings. The more you can pick up on the feelings of others, through the verbal and nonverbal signals they send, the better you'll be able to understand what's driving the behaviors you're seeing in the meeting. An empathetic person has an orientation toward service to others, a keen understanding of what others need to progress and develop, along with political awareness, whereby they are able to read the emotional current and power dynamics in any group.

Empathy is the foundation of emotional intelligence. Empathy is about how well you're able to be in somebody else's shoes, to take the time and energy to understand what they need, what they want, and how they want it. You'll likely be familiar with the golden rule: *do unto others as you would have them do unto you.* There's the 2.0 version of that, the platinum rule: *treat others as **they** would like to be treated.* They might not wish to be treated the same way you like to be treated. How do you find out how they want to be treated? By scheduling one-on-one meetings with your team and making time to find out.

I believe that most people have good hearts and good intentions. But what happens when the heat gets turned up, and expectations and pressure increase while timelines decrease? Things get overwhelming. People work overtime. They get tired. Seemingly small things can set someone off. This is when people don't show up at their best on the emotional side—because they're being driven on the technical side. They've got to produce results, and so paying attention to this "people stuff"—listening, taking time to be kind, responding versus reacting, checking in with your team—that becomes secondary.

As facilitators, when we walk into the meeting room we don't really know what people are up against, what's happening in their lives outside of work, where they came from, what their life is like, what challenges they're experiencing at work. When we find ourselves in a situation that's becoming dysfunctional, we can serve our team and the person dealing with challenges by being on the playing field *with* them.

With empathy we offer a path off the field on which they became side-tracked—the field that isn't serving them, the team or the session objective. We dig down deep to the place where we're all human.

Empathy drives you to check in with the dysfunctional person during a break, calmly and thoughtfully even when they've been acting like a jerk, to find out where they're at, what's going on, and how you can help. People stop participating in meetings because of all sorts of situational and external things that have nothing to do with the meeting.

I recently had a participant come in late to a morning meeting, looking agitated and annoyed.

"Are we *still* taking about this? How long is it going to take for us to *finally* make a decision here? There will always be more data to analyze. C'mon, you've got to do something. Now!"

People shifted in their seats, another teammate spoke up. "Geez Steve, what's *your* problem?"

"My *problem* is my mom, Jason. I've been up all night with her. And I came in to be at this meeting because I thought this decision had to be made today and I needed to be here. As soon as the meeting is over, I'm going right back to the hospital."

This is a call for empathy.

"Oh Steve, we're so sorry. Thank you for being this committed to the team. How can we help? "

"Well thanks. Sorry I'm so short. I'm tired. There's nothing to do right now. Thanks though."

After the meeting the team got together for a quick huddle and put together a meal chain. Everyone signed up to bring dinner to Steve and his family every other day for the next two weeks. That's empathy.

5. Social Skills.

Social skills are the skills involved in creating, building, and maintaining relationships. Building relationships in business is critical, and it takes great interpersonal skills. Yup, I'm talking people skills again. Those with strong social skills are able to communicate clearly, influence and persuade, inspire and guide, effectively manage change, understand how to resolve conflict and reach agreements, cooperate and collaborate, and create the foundations for teams and groups to pursue common goals. We use the other four EQ factors to increase our social skills capacity.

Roots and Fruits

Imagine a fruit tree. What's underneath? If the tree is planted in rich, loamy soil that's laden with nutrients, you'll see bright, healthy fruits bursting with goodness dangling from the tree's limbs. If the roots are being fed poison, or all the nutrients in the soil have been leached out, or if the tree has been planted in the wrong environment, what kind of fruit will you see?

Think of self-awareness, self-regulation, motivation, and empathy as the roots. And the social skills are the fruits. What are you feeding your roots? Check out your fruits!

TWENTY-ONE

Music

---

*M*usic and meetings? You bet. Music is a fantastic tool to help set the tone you want for the meeting. I'm not talking about blaring Led Zeppelin while you're analyzing the quarterly financial report. I'm talking about playing music before the meeting starts, during breaks, and during small group break-out work.

Music fills in that awkward silence as people begin arriving for your session. It sends the nonverbal message, "Hey, come on in, relax, everything is A-okay." It pumps up both you and the team. Music works magic on the brain. It evokes memory and emotion. The first thing I do when I walk in the room is set up my portable speaker and get my music on. I get my game going, get myself revved up. I get myself in the right mental state using music as the stimulus. The music plays until the start time. When the music stops, it's a signal to the participants: we're ready to go.

Your choice of music will be dictated by the type of meeting you're having. Here are some song ideas for your playlist:

> *"Lovely Day"* — *Bill Withers*
> *"Everyday"* — *Dave Matthews*
> *"Morning Dance"* — *Spyro Gyra*
> *"Mr. Blue Sky"* — *ELO*

"One Fine Morning" — Lighthouse
"Overkill" (acoustic) — Colin Hay
"Pride and Joy" — Stevie Ray Vaughn (This one's a rocker.)
"Sail on, Sailor" — The Beach Boys
"Slippery People" — Talking Heads
"Steady On" — Shawn Colvin
"Electric Feel" — MGMT
"Everybody Is a Star" — Sly & the Family Stone
"Got to Give It Up" — Marvin Gaye
"Here Comes the Sun" (live) — Richie Havens
"Higher Ground" — Stevie Wonder
"I Say a Little Prayer" — Aretha Franklin
"In the Mood" — Glen Miller
"It's Not Unusual" — Tom Jones
"Fly Me to the Moon" — Frank Sinatra
(And you can add many more!)

Songs to Avoid

I facilitated a meeting not so long ago with the session objective to downsize the company 10 percent. There were forty positions being eliminated and forty people who were going to be out of a job. Looking over the playlist during the prework, I made sure I took "Celebrate" by Kool & the Gang off the list. Make sense? Nor did I want the sad songs with lyrics such as, "…nothing left to live for…" The point is to know your session objective and choose the music accordingly.

Choose a variety, from top forty to country, jazz, classic rock, and rap (without offensive lyrics). Pick songs you like—you'll have more fun setting up and recharging at breaks!

Ask Forgiveness Not Permission

One of the things I've learned about bringing music to meetings is to ask for forgiveness, not permission. Early on in my career, in prework meetings, I'd discuss playing music for the meeting and would immediately get pushback. "Music? Why? We don't do that here. That's not really professional." The looks on some faces said, "What kind of facilitator are you?" The idea of music let loose a lot of questions that didn't need to be there in my clients' minds. I learned a good lesson. So, for the last couple of decades, I've been bringing the music and turning it on, and I've never had anybody tell me to turn it off. I *have* had people say, "Hey, what's with the music? We don't usually do that here." And I say, "Well, I'd be happy to tell you about that. Is now a good time?" Usually they say, "No, that's okay."

If this happens to you, only they say that now is a good time to discuss it, here's your script.

> *Music is a tool to create the context for our meeting environment. There's a ton of research on the effect music has on setting the tone and tapping into the creative side of the brain, which we will really need for our work today! I've got a big playlist. Requests?*

So far I haven't had to ask for forgiveness. I'll keep you posted.

Adding music goes a long way to building teams. That's been my lesson learned. Someone walks in the room, and says, "Oh! I haven't heard this song in so long. I remember that time when I..." And then somebody across the table, who might not have struck up a conversation with that person before, says, "Yes, I remember that, too. Do you remember...?" It starts conversations. Music is tied to memory and emotion, as I said before, and it's a really good way to warm up a group. Some people are nervous walking into a big room—their boss might be there, or the objective might be emotionally charged. Music fills in the gap, sets the tone, and even makes your meetings fun!

Section V: Addressing Dysfunction

TWENTY-TWO

Addressing Dysfunction

*H*ave you ever been white-water rafting, or seen pictures of it? Skillfully facilitating a team is a lot like being a white-water rafting guide. All you need are a few reliable tools: a sturdy boat, paddles and guiding skills to navigate your boat through the most turbulent waters and keep your team safe. Setting out from shore, you sit up on your frame so you can scan for obstacles and stay on course.

How do we keep the team together no matter how turbulent the water we find ourselves in? How do we keep the team safely in the boat when someone is poking holes in it? What about the person trying to throw someone overboard? Or the seemingly friendly, helpful person who suddenly tries to knock you off your seat, take the paddles and—*mutiny*!

Managing dysfunctional behavior is a fear many facilitators have. Without skills and training the very idea of addressing dysfunction during your meeting can feel like purposely guiding your raft into the rapids and taking it over a waterfall.

Dysfunction comes in many forms: whispering, texting, falling asleep, rudeness, challenges to authority, and verbal attacks. Handling team dysfunction can be a challenge, especially if the dysfunctional person is the boss. One thing we know for sure: if the dysfunction is not addressed it will continue, and sometimes escalate. In your role as facilitator it's up to you to take action.

The good news is that with just a few reliable tools, which I will provide you with in this section, you can skillfully navigate any obstacle you find along your meeting journey.

Effectively addressing dysfunction involves three parts.

1. Prevention. This begins with prework.
2. Early detection. Engaging your energy and emotional intelligence will equip you with early detection skills.
3. Clean resolution. This where the T-E-A-M approach resides, and much of it happens through expert use of open-ended questions.

Prevention

Save yourself a boatload of time, energy and heartache by *preventing* dysfunction. Yes, we're back to the prework! A lot of the dysfunction you experience in meetings comes from winging it. Hoping things will go okay is not an effective meeting-facilitation strategy. Learning about issues that might impact achieving the session objective, and about potential conflicts within the team, before the meeting begins, gives you time to course correct and avoid confusion and conflicts in the session. Do the prework.

Early Detection.

In your prework, and especially in the meeting, keep your radar on high to detect dysfunction early and then take effective action quickly. Because so much of communication is nonverbal, you'll want to scan your group, keeping your eyes and ears open for what's going on in the room over and above the verbal discussion.

The early warning signs of dysfunction are usually nonverbal. People will show their discomfort through their physical actions and facial expressions long before they actually say anything. Watch for these signs:

- Shifting in seats
- Seats moving away from the table
- Crossed arms, in a tense way
- Rolling eyes
- Loud sighs, huffs and tsk, tsk sounds
- Snorts, giggles
- Silence and disengagement
- Nudging neighbors
- Walking out
- Coming in late, leaving early
- Rapid clicking of pens
- Rubbing temples
- Head down in hands
- Sleeping
- Doing other work.

Once you've detected the early signs of dysfunction, address the behavior before it escalates. Move into clean resolution using the T-E-A-M approach.

T-E-A-M

Addressing dysfunction cleanly, respectfully, and in a way that results in resolution is a four-step process that spells the word *team*.

Step 1: T=Take Action

Step 2: E=(With) Empathy

Step 3: A=(Seek an) Agreement

Step 4: M=Move On

Unless done properly, the facilitator's attempts to address dysfunction will often be perceived by teams as conflict. Conflict prompts defensiveness. We operate differently when we're defensive. As the facilitator, it's *how* we take action that really counts.

Step 1: Take Action

Take action early. A tiny fire can be put out with a cup of water and the gentle kick of a boot. If you wait, it can build into an all-consuming inferno. Enter into this interaction as though it were a friendly chat, whether you're addressing the whole group generally or you're meeting with someone privately. This is not a parent-to-child conversation. No scolding involved in words or tone. Engage your emotional intelligence.

Taking action happens in two levels and with empathy woven right in.

1. Addressing the group generally. This is a level one intervention.
2. Addressing someone privately. This is a level two intervention involving talking to a specific person one-to-one at a break.

Addressing the Group Generally

This is our first level intervention. You're addressing the entire team, and no one is being called out individually. Think of it as a friendly reminder from the facilitator to the team. Addressing the group works well for typical meeting interruptions that aren't emotionally charged. Here are three ways to address dysfunction within the general group.

- **Use the power of proximity**: Walking toward people and physically moving into their space gets their attention on a subconscious level. The U-shaped table setup makes this easy to do. Walking toward the whisperer, the story teller who tends to go on and on, or the dominant speaker may be all you need to do. Coming into their space is an effective nonverbal cue for them to stop and self-correct their course. When you're facilitating, be sure to take the occasional spin into the U as discussions are happening throughout the meeting. This way, when you do need to use the power of proximity to address dysfunction no one will even know what you're doing. And you don't even have to say a word. Low risk for you and it works like magic.

- **Refer to the agreements**: In your prework you will have set the foundation for your meeting by identifying and communicating to the team the context of your session. Having the five pillars (session objective, agenda, agreements, consensus decision-making, and parking lot) posted on the wall at the front of the room serves as your safety net to manage behaviors during the meeting. If you aren't able to move in the U and use the power of proximity, or you used it and the behavior continues, refer to the agreements to quickly address the general group in a level one intervention. In the script below, I show how to address whispering without calling out anyone by name. When you notice whispering, point to the agreements chart and jump right in, with a smile and a neutral tone. Use this script for texting as well. Insert the "electronics off" agreement. Remember, this is a friendly chat. And you just let everyone know you're paying attention, you will take action, and there are boundaries in place to maintain a professional, respectful environment.

Hey everyone! A friendly reminder: in our agreements we covered whispering right here in "respect the speaker". We're all still on board, yes? (People nod their heads.)

Great! Thanks. Let's keep going. We're talking about...

- **Check in:** Think back to meetings you've been in, where the discussion was going along and then *something* changed. The energy in the room shifted. It got quiet, people started looking down, doodling on their papers, and you weren't quite sure what just happened. Trust your gut. This is your cue to *check in*. Checking in has two parts:

1. Tell the team what you're noticing.
2. Ask an open-ended question.

> *Hey everybody, I want to check in. Feels like we were rolling along and then something shifted. What about you? What do you think just happened?*

Sometimes the team will say, "No, nothing, we're thinking," or, "We're getting tired," then move on. If they're tired, take a break.

You might hear, "Well since you asked, contract negotiations are coming up and this is a tender topic…"

Making time, even fifteen minutes, to allow some venting of concerns and clarify what can done in *this* session about *that* concern or issue, whatever it may be, can be enough to clear the air and allow the team to refocus and continue forward.

When a long-standing issue, or an issue that cannot be addressed in your session, is revealed by checking in, suggest this topic be put in the parking lot and follow up with how and when it could be addressed outside the meeting.

In all cases, when you address the general group to identify potential dysfunction by using the checking in facilitator superpower, you demonstrate your laser-like attention to all communication in the room, verbal and nonverbal, and your willingness to facilitate discussions on any topic that will remove obstacles and support the group in achieving their session objective. Checking in demonstrates empathy, care, and kindness, the noble qualities of exceptional leadership.

When you address behaviors early and gently as we do in this first level intervention, the team takes note and self regulates their behavior. No one wants to sit through meetings that suck. Your intervention demonstrates your commitment to an efficient session and the team raises their own performance bar in kind.

Addressing Someone Privately

Let's say addressing the general group isn't working. You've walked into the U-shaped setup toward the whisperer, you've referred to the agreements including "respect the speaker," and the person just keeps whispering. Bless their hearts. It's time for a level two intervention.

Take a break and address the whisperer privately. (This is another reason why we don't put times on the agenda posted at the front of the room: it gives us the flexibility to take breaks as needed.) Talk to the whisperer in a place that is as private as possible, away from others.

Remember to enter into this interaction as though it were a friendly chat. Treat this person as a professional expert. Here's the formula you can use to address someone privately. Sometimes you will use all the steps, sometimes you won't.

- Call a break and go over to the person for a private chat.
- Ask an open-ended question.
- Define your role.
- Describe the behavior.
- Seek agreement (the A in T-E-A-M).
- Ask open-ended questions.
- Confirm agreement.
- Move on (the M in T-E-A-M).
- Say thanks.

Each interaction will be a bit different. Later in this chapter I'll share a full script that you can R&D (rip off and duplicate) and use in your sessions.

You might not be able to solve the big problem at the break, but you can put the tourniquet on and see how it goes. Sometimes it's enough to slow somebody's negative energy and settle their emotions. In some cases, I've gotten a lot of traction with people without saying a word. I've just listened.

Step 2: Empathy

Taking action to address dysfunction effectively always involves the right-brain skill of empathy. It's woven into every step of T-E-A-M. You'll recall from Section IV that empathy is one part of our emotional intelligence. It's about *how* and *who* you're *being* with your team.

What does your team need from you?

I was watching a news segment about a U.S. Army officer and his team in Afghanistan.

The video showed the leader assisting medics as they were loading the wounded from his battalion into the back of a C-141 transport plane. Heads, arms, and legs, all wrapped in gauze, IV bags dangling. They were being flown to a trauma center for treatment. He hopped from one gurney to the next, whispering words of encouragement and gently touching them on the cheek, the shoulder—and then, the commander bent over to kiss each one on the forehead.

Moving. Amazing. Leadership and love in action.

People come into meetings carrying a lot of stuff. We could say metaphorical wounds. Stuff from outside work, inside work, their personal relationships, their families. They will bring emotions into your meetings, and those emotions will drive their behavior.

Taking action from a place of empathy can remove obstacles and expand the very best qualities in you and your team.

How can you build your capacity to facilitate and lead with empathy—and even love?

Monitor your own emotions.

Engaging in private meetings to address dysfunction can be stressful. These interactions can trigger your emotions and cause you to react rather than respond, especially when you're doing this in a short break at your meeting.

The following are signs that you're not meeting the individual with empathy:

- You find yourself trying to change their mind about how they're feeling.

- You get into a conversation about why what they're feeling doesn't make sense to you.
- You encourage them to "get over it."

Don't try to talk people out of what they're feeling. "I don't know why you're so angry. This is not that big of a deal." Or, "Why don't you just calm down and not get so worked up (or emotional). Just listen to the facts and keep an open mind."

These approaches are like throwing gas on a fire. The dysfunctional person is left feeling unheard and the emotion they're feeling actually escalates. Your responses will only drive the person's feelings underground, and they will resurface to bite you later.

The key is to combine empathy and compassion with open-ended questions. It's all connected. Get curious: what are *they* feeling and experiencing? Acknowledge what they're feeling. Here's a sample exchange:

How's the meeting going for you?

"I don't like it."

What's happening?

"This is exactly what happened last time. It's not going to work."

That sounds frustrating. (Or insert the word or words they've used.)

"Frustrating? Yeah. This is a complete waste of time!"

I hear that. How can I help?

Meet them where they are. If they're mad, they're mad. Even if we don't understand it, it's not our job to change their minds about how they are feeling or convince them otherwise. Our job is to clarify the behavior that is causing a disruption and to support them as they decide how they will change their behavior, so they can go back into the meeting and participate in a way that brings value to the team.

Step 3: Agreement

Ask open-ended questions (what, why, how) that get them talking about ways they might see themselves being able to function in their subject-matter expert role. It's about having them work their way through their issue to come up with the thing that will become the source of the agreement, as opposed to you forcing an agreement on them.

- What do you think would help at this point?
- How do you see yourself participating in the meeting in your role as subject-matter expert?
- What do you see as a solution at this point?
- How can I help?
- What do you want to happen? What is your goal?
- How do you see what you're doing now helping you get what you want?

Remember, empathy will help you get to that agreement—the 'A' in T-E-A-M—a lot faster.

No Agreement?

If the above steps don't result in an agreement, suggest meeting again at the next break.

Since we don't have more time during this break, how about we press pause on this and talk more at the next break?

Escalation

If their emotion escalates or they become combative, shut this behavior down.

> *Feels like this may not be a good fit for you. Who would you suggest we talk to about this? We'll need to get another subject-matter expert in the room to fill your role.*

You may need to go back into the room as break is wrapping up to let the team know.

> *Hey team, thanks for getting back from break on time. We've had some unforeseen issues come up that need immediate attention. We will be taking an extended break. Thanks for your understanding. See you in thirty minutes...*

If this is an hour-long meeting, you might just say that the meeting is done for the day, apologize for the disruption, and let the team know you'll reschedule.

Step 4: Move On

Human beings are fascinating. The same team can show up differently for every meeting. Your star performers will have a bad day now and again. People who are pessimists may surprise you and show up energized, full of ideas.

Dysfunction reveals itself in a wide range of behaviors. Some are easy to navigate. Some are unexpected. And some are huge, like a giant rock or a log jam. Like the white-water rafting guide, you adapt to the conditions as they emerge. The river changes constantly and you address whatever is coming your way; you navigate around obstacles so the raft stays afloat, the team stays intact, and you move on.

Conflict can be uncomfortable. The team looks to you for their cues on how to move on. Was that set of rapids we just went through exhilarating? Terrifying? Both? How is the outburst by that team member, which led us to take a break, going to make the rest of the meeting feel when we reconvene?

You set the context for them. How you move on shows them the way. How are you showing up after addressing dysfunction generally or privately? Annoyed, flustered, low energy? Our goal is clean resolution. Be focused, professional, and responsible for the energy you bring into the room.

Guiding the boat through the churning water of addressing dysfunctional behavior will take all your focus and skill on the technical side and the people side.

Keep breathing. Stay focused. Do your prework, rehearse the scripts. When you feel you're veering off course, take action early to get back on track.

Be good to yourself. This is not easy work. I'm sending you a virtual, over-the-head-with-both-hands high five. You've got this! And know that being willing to enter into the big rapids will help you stretch and grow in the finest ways. Enjoy the ride.

The T-E-A-M Script

I want you to see all four steps of T-E-A-M unfold in a single, uninterrupted script. You'll want to rehearse this script out loud until it feels comfortable and familiar, so it really does seem like a friendly chat when you use it. For this script, the dysfunctional behavior is whispering. We've just called a break and you are going over to address the whisperer privately.

Hi, got a minute? (Take action.)

"Sure."

How's the meeting going for you? (Open-ended question, with empathy.)

"Fine." (Or, they may give you their story about how they see the meeting.)

What are you seeing? How do you think we're doing?

"I think things are going well. This is a good team. I wanted to let you know that my daughter is home sick from school today, so I might have to leave early."

(Taking a moment to listen to them will build rapport.)

> *Okay, thanks for the heads-up. Hope she is doing okay?*
> (Empathy)

"Yah, she's got a bad cold, nothing serious."

> *I wanted to check in with you. In my role as facilitator I make sure we stay on track and focused and I've noticed you've been whispering.* (Define your role and describe the behavior.)

> *I'm wondering how I can help. What questions might you have?*

"No, I'm good. I was whispering to my teammate that we had come up with ideas about how to solve this just last week."

> *Oh, good. That will be helpful as we move forward. For right now, the whispering part. We talked about whispering in the agreements when we began the meeting, and I've referred to them during our discussion. The whispering is distracting and takes us off track. How can I help you with that?* (Seek agreement.)

"Oh, sorry, I can stop."

Thanks, I appreciate your holding the whispering. (Confirm
   agreement.)

*Great. And please jot down your ideas. We don't want to miss
   them when we get to solutions later today! Thanks again. See
   you after break.* (Move on.)

On one end of the spectrum, it can be that easy. On the other end
of the spectrum, you'll find participants whose behavior escalates.
They will begin to resist or derail the process. This is where you need
empathy the most, and where it can be most difficult to give. Think of
it as a great opportunity to practice expanding your emotional intelligence.

Hi, got a minute? (Take action.)

"Sure."

How's the meeting going for you? (Empathy.)

"This is a complete waste of time. We've tried to fix this at least
twice."

Sounds frustrating. What can I do to help? (Empathy.)

"Without leadership's support here, I think we're doomed. I've
seen this over and over again. I've been here for twenty-four years.
New leaders swap in and out every three to four years. They come in
with their new promises and initiatives, then a few years later, they're
gone and everything we've worked on gets scrapped. Then we're on to
the next flavor of the month. It's really disappointing."

*Yes, frustrating! I'm sorry. What can we do for now, so you can
   go back in the meeting in your role as subject-matter expert?*
   (Empathy and seeking agreement.)

"You can get me off this team."

> *Well we won't be able to do that in the time we have left on this break. So, for now, how can I help?*

"Well, there's nothing we can do about it right now. We're doomed."

> *How about I check in with you at the next break to see how things are going and we can talk more about what to do next?* (Temporary agreement.)

"Okay."

> *Thanks. With all of your experience, please jump in with ideas, things you see working going forward. You have an important perspective, and the team knows that you know what you're talking about on these technical issues.* (Move on.)

"Yeah, sure."

A Recap

There is a lot of information in this chapter. Let's look it over as a quick review from the thirty-thousand-foot level. The three parts to successfully addressing dysfunction are:

1. Prevention

- Do your prework.
- Early detection. Remember, the first signs of dysfunction are nonverbal. Look for those nonverbal cues.

2. Address the Whole Group (Level One Intervention)

- Use the power of proximity (use the U-shaped setup).
- Refer to the agreements (posted at the front of the room).
- Check in. This has two parts—tell the team what you noticed, and ask them what it means.

3. Address Privately (Level Two Intervention)

- T: Take action. Call a break.
- E: Empathy. Set your intention for a friendly chat.
- A: Agreement. Use open-ended questions to support the person in deciding to change their behavior.
- M: Move on. Keep the boat moving forward and get the meeting back on course.

TWENTY-THREE

The Storyteller

*H*ow you address dysfunctional behavior depends on what kind of dysfunction it is, and who or what the source is. Different types of characters, or personalities, find their way into every meeting. Left unchecked, the behavior of these characters can quickly descend into dysfunction. As facilitator, it will be your job to spot the signs early and gently redirect to keep the team on track and the session objective in focus. The next several chapters delve into these different characters and personalities that are common in meetings and lay out an approach to address the dysfunction they may bring with them into the meeting.

Let's start with the storyteller.

The storyteller is often a long-time employee, or they've been working in their field for a long time. They have lots of stories. They've seen everything that's happened, both good and bad. Their comment or story in the team discussion refers to something ten or twenty years in the past. And it takes a long time for them to get to the point.

The rest of the team, familiar with this behavior, often loses patience with the storyteller. They'll roll their eyes and huff and sigh. They might even utter, "Oh, here we go again!"

Unfortunately, if the storyteller's style of disruptive behavior isn't managed properly, the golden nuggets of history and experience they bring are lost. The team tunes out when the storyteller begins. As facilitator, it can be difficult to know when to interrupt the story because there may be some important information in it that the team can actually use. It's tricky. How do you keep the team focused during the story? And how do you help the storyteller get to the point without hurting or embarrassing them?

The storyteller may have trouble wrapping words around their main idea. They have a *big* idea and a long timeline. When they start to speak about it, you can see their face shift. They're thinking as they talk, verbally processing, working to put words to something new, or to something that they've not spoken aloud before.

Fear of Public Speaking

Often the storyteller hasn't yet had a chance to tell the story or hasn't felt listened to. For many people, public speaking is a huge fear, so when it's their turn to speak or it's their opportunity to share what they know, they get nervous. Everyone is looking at them, the boss is sitting right there, their fight-or-flight response gets activated, their access to the thinking part of their brain is derailed, and they lose track of their story. They don't want to look stupid, so they keep going and going. When emotions go up, intelligence goes down.

What if the boss is the storyteller? Nobody wants to interrupt *the boss*. So, the boss goes on and on and on. Out of a misguided sense of respect, or fear, no one knows what to do.

Your first cue that you have a storyteller is a *feeling* you notice. It's sense of, "Uh-oh, where are we going?" Do a quick scan of the room— you may be getting nonverbal cues from the team (eye rolling or sighs). After you get *the feeling* from the storyteller, you need to take action.

The Headline

What do you do? You're going to take action with a tool called *the headline.*

First, we're going to assume that good prework was done. That means the team knows that, in your role as facilitator, you may interrupt in order to keep the team on track and that you'll do so in a respectful way.

1. Adjust your face. Make sure you have a pleasant little smile showing—because next you're going to use the power of proximity and walk from the front of the room toward the storyteller. People will be watching you. What they will see first is your smile, your nonverbal cue that everything is okay.

2. Move to the inside of the U-shaped table. Position yourself in front of the storyteller.

3. They're going to look up at you, because you'll be right in their space, and will usually continue talking.

4. Within a few seconds, they'll take a breath, a pause to get more air to keep their story going. Use this physical gesture to get their attention and focus: raise both hands up like parentheses, and say, *Imagine your idea as a headline, across the top of a newspaper, five to seven words. What would the headline say?*

5. The storyteller will pause. They won't know what their headline is. That's your signal to get them some sticky notes. You say, *Hey! Give Chris some sticky notes.*

6. Take the sticky-note pad that's being handed over and say, *Chris, take a moment. Get that idea into a headline, and I'll be right back with you.* Big smile on your face.

7. Return to the front of the room and do a quick review of what's already been talked about. Perhaps the discussion is being recorded on the chart at the front of the room where the team's sticky notes with their other ideas are displayed.

8. *So, the last two items we were talking about were A and B. We've got Chris working on his idea. We'll get right back to him. What else do we want to talk about around this idea of solutions for XYZ?* And you keep going.

9. At the end of that agenda item, check back with Chris and say, *Chris, how's that headline?* And more times than not, I've heard the storyteller say, "Yup, we've got it already. It's good. You covered it." If you haven't covered it, grab the sticky note and put it up on the chart, or wherever the recording is happening.

It's *how* you take action. You take action with empathy and respect, with a smile on your face—a physical and visual gesture to support the storyteller in crystalizing the concept, saving face, adding their idea, and shifting their brain into quick focus.

During a recent two-day training session I was leading, we were practicing the headline method of intervention.

About forty minutes in, one of the most-engaged participants, Mary, asked a question that quickly turned into a story.

"So I was remembering this meeting I was in. Well actually it happens a lot on one of the teams I'm a part of—this person always asks about things, lots of different things, that are not on the agenda. Like, one time they asked about how a process that was implemented a decade ago was like the one we were implementing now. And it was weird because she was on that project so why is she asking me this now, as she should know…"

Mary continued for another fifteen seconds or so. I smiled and began to slowly walk over to her. Some of the other participants noticed what was happening, live and in color. *The headline.* I used the script.

Mary, imagine this idea like a headline, five to seven words…

She paused. I asked for the sticky-note pad.

*Mary, take a moment and get your idea down in a headline and
I'll get right back to you.*

She took the sticky-note pad and began to work on her idea.

Okay team, questions on the headline?

The other participants were smiling, looking at each other.
Someone asked Mary if she knew what had just happened. She said,
"Hang on, I'm writing."

The class conducted a quick debrief of the headline intervention
technique I'd just demonstrated. Mary was still puzzled. It took her a
few moments to realize what had happened.

"Oh, my goodness, I was the storyteller, and you did the headline!"

Boom. That's how smooth that is. Like butter in a hot pan. People
don't even know it's happening, even when we've just been talking
about it as a technique.

Extremes and Escalation

I've had people who are really committed to their story, and who want
to hold the floor and finish it. I've seen people lean sideways into the
person sitting next to them to keep talking to the whole group, as
though I weren't standing there in front of them. In that case, assess
what's going on in the room. What's your sense of how the group is
feeling? Will you give them thirty more seconds, and then attempt
another headline, or is it time to shut this down, call a break, and talk
to the storyteller privately? (By this time, you're really glad you
haven't posted times on your agenda. You have the flexibility to take
breaks whenever you need to, and you'll always be on time.
No drama.)

Let's talk about what to do when you encounter the extreme storyteller and your headline intervention hasn't worked. You'll call a break
and address them privately.

Hi, hey how's the meeting going for you?

"It's fine, I'm trying to get my ideas heard. Seems like you want to shut me down."

> *Oh, I'm sorry it felt like that. In my role as facilitator, I want to make sure we stay right on track. My intention is to offer a moment, for you in this case, to take a big idea with lots of parts and condense it so the discussion can keep moving.*

"Yeah. I get it. I'm not dumb. You want me to shut up."

> *I'm sorry you heard "shut up." My intention was to support you. (Slow this conversation way down.) Have you ever been in a meeting and someone is telling a story and you get lost, not sure where it's going?* (Pause.)

> *I was getting that feeling and saw some cues from the group that suggested they might be feeling that too. And I want to make sure everybody gets a turn. I didn't want us to miss your idea, so that's why I asked for a headline. A bullet point or two.*

"Well, whatever."

> *How can I help now?*

"I'm fine."

> *Did you get a chance to get your ideas down into bullet points?*

"I did."

> *How about you give them to me and I'll put them up on the board?*

"Okay."

Thanks.

You're implementing the E in T-E-A-M: empathy. Did they hear or feel, "shut up"? Yes, they did. What is your objective? To reach an agreement on how they will amend their behavior. You're not going to get any traction fighting, disputing whether you said shut up or not. ("I did NOT say 'shut up'." "Yes, you did." "No. I didn't.") So, go with them. They heard, or felt, "shut up."

Here's an additional way to explain your facilitator role.

> *I'm sorry you heard "shut up." My intention was to make sure that we stay on track and focused, as we talked about in the prework before the meeting. In my role as facilitator, sometimes I jump in and use the headline as a way to help condense a story or idea. I want to save time and keep the team focused. I'm not asking you to shut up. I want to make sure everybody gets a turn.*

"Yes. I get it."

> *I'd love to hear from you, and I want to make sure everyone else gets in the discussion. What can I do to do help?*

"Nothing, I got it."

Sometimes after you conduct this private intervention and we come back from break, the storyteller won't talk. One extreme to the other. For now, that's okay. And for now, let them lick their wounds. You've given them a salve, you've apologized. It's now on them to decide how they want to behave. Occasionally someone may sulk. They can choose to sulk, if they want, as long as they don't get in the way of what you're trying to achieve. Engage your emotional intelligence and remain compassionate and empathetic. Nobody enjoys getting called out by the facilitator, even if it is in private.

Respectful Interruption

When I'm training new facilitators on how to implement the headline, there's always a question about respect. "Isn't it rude to interrupt? Isn't it disrespectful not to let them finish?"

This is a great opportunity to define roles and expectations, to introduce the tools that will be used to manage the team dynamics, and to talk about how the prework helps to create respectful boundaries in meetings. And it leads us into an important discussion of whether it's respectful to five, ten, or twenty people in a meeting to be held hostage by one member's inability to get to the point. As the facilitator, am I being respectful to the rest of the team by *not* intervening? People going on and on is consistently reported as one of the behaviors that drives people crazy in meetings. It's one big reason meetings can suck. In facilitation and leadership training this discussion is a great opportunity to examine one's relationship to conflict, and to examine the culture and norms of an organization.

How much is everyone's time worth? How important is it that we achieve the session objective? How important is it that we begin and end on time? It's important. Practice your headline.

TWENTY-FOUR

The Repeater

---

*T*he repeater is the one who makes the same point over and over. "We can't do that because..." You'll carry on with the meeting, and then a few minutes later they'll raise their hand again and say, "Yeah, but we can't do that because of ..."

Your intervention involves finding the repeated comment wherever it has been recorded on the easel chart pad.

> *Looks like we've covered it here, here, and here it is again, yes?*

"Yeah, but..." And they repeat their point again.

> *So, what about these three things and what you're saying now is different? The same? What haven't we covered? I want to make sure you get heard.*

"Well, okay, you got it, it's just really important."

> *Yes, understood. I'm confirming that your idea/concern is duly noted. Great, and now, let's keep moving forward. How's that sound? (Tone and tempo are key here. Speak slowly and respectfully.)*

If the repeater now says, "Well, it's kind of the same, but I was thinking that in addition it's kind of like..." And they trail off into thinking out loud. That's your cue for the headline.

> *Get Jason the sticky notes. Here you go, Jason. Take a moment and get your idea into a bullet point, like a headline across the top of a newspaper. Thank you and I'll get right back to you. I want to make sure we have your idea fully covered here.*

Another approach is to give them the floor for a set amount of time.

> *Jason, team, sounds like there are some details you want to make sure we've recorded. How about three full minutes? I can set the timer for three minutes. You have the floor. Finish everything that you have left to say about this. And then, how about we agree to move on? How would that be?*

"Yeah, because there's this one piece everybody's missing."

> *How is that, everybody?*

Usually the team agrees because the promise is that they will only have to listen for three more minutes. You give the repeater the floor, and they say their piece. Sometimes that's all it takes, and they move on. Sometimes people simply need to feel that they have been heard. Once they get their point across, they—and you—can move on.

If they aren't able to stop after the timer goes off, take a break for a level-two intervention and have a private conversation.

> *Checking in with you. I'm a bit confused. I believe we've covered your idea/concern. We have it listed on the chart several times. I'm noticing you've come back to it again. I'm wondering how I can help, so we can continue to move forward, rather than take time to rewind?*

Then you listen. They might tell you they're concerned that not everyone understands. Or that this is *so* important. Time to tap into empathy tempered with boundaries.

> *What do you need to feel heard? What would it look like and*
> *sound like to feel heard?*

Then you decide whether their request is possible. Sometimes the repeater wants the team to adopt their idea, and if the conversation doesn't seem to be moving in that direction, they repeat the idea with more evidence of why it's best.

> *Hey, it looks like this isn't the number-one idea with the team.*
> *How are you going to manage yourself when we get back in*
> *the room if this idea doesn't fly with the whole team? I know*
> *your idea has value—you see value in it, and I'm sure others*
> *do too. And* (note the use of "and," not "but") *it may*
> *not be the one selected. So how do you see yourself adapting to*
> *that? Because we're spending a lot of time rewinding to this*
> *idea. It seems like most of the group acknowledges your idea*
> *and they are interested in discussing other options and ideas*
> *as well.*

If there are several people getting on board with the repeater's idea, or, conversely, most of the team seems opposed to the repeater's idea, that's important information for us as facilitators. Why?

Beware of group think, where teams can get in their own way. They get stuck on an anticipated path and interpret the data in a way that supports the path. They may get excited about the idea, or in some cases, they just want the decision to be made so they can move on. In this mindset, really important information can get overlooked—especially if the person suggesting an idea is somebody who has a reputation for disruption. People won't give the same weight to the idea. They'll just want to blow off the repeater.

"Wah-wah. Jason is always complaining."

I've seen teams do a complete turn-around from the direction they were heading when they finally give the person (or people) who really dug in on their idea a chance to be heard. In cases like this, it isn't about the repeater trying to sabotage, or wanting their own way, or some kind of an emotional thing. The repeater has tons of technical data on which they're basing their concerns and ideas. If we facilitate the space for them to be heard, the information can be invaluable to the team and result in a different outcome than the one originally beginning to materialize.

> *Wait a minute everybody. I'm curious about Jason's perspective. He's been here a long time. He's seen lots of changes—what's worked and what hasn't. What do you say we take just a few minutes, clear our mental screens, and listen, really listen, for information that could impact the direction we're taking?*
> *And Jason, I hear your concern about this idea and direction, and the circling back to it several times. What is it? What are the things concerning you? What are we missing?*

Allow Jason to be seen, not as a problem, but as an important contributor. Allow Jason to speak.

> *Thanks Jason. Now, team, how does this information inform our path forward? Your thoughts?*

The team may decide to continue as planned, they may make a course correction, or they may completely change course.

What absolutely does happen is Jason's being heard and acknowledged. It sets a standard of respect for the whole team. More ideas are shared when people know they will be listened to. If that's how you treat Jason, that's how you'll treat them.

Now, if the discussion feels like it's moving in a direction out of exasperation or domination, that's a call for us as facilitators to pause and say, "What's going on here? What is this about? How is this going to benefit the team?"

If it's information that the team needs to hear, how do you make that happen? Stop the discussion. Ask the team open-ended questions.

> *Hey team, I want to check in here. Let's do a quick review of where we've been and where we're going. Looking back at our discussion (refer to the charts and sticky notes) we were talking about A, B, C. Shelley began adding her ideas here and it looks like we're changing course. I want to confirm we understand the data, and this is the direction you're willing to go. Talk to me.*

Wait for someone to speak. It may be Shelley.

> *Thanks for that, Shelley. Let's hear from others. I want to make sure we're not feeling pushed to go a certain way. Or perhaps you're getting a little tired and want to be done. I get that, and let's be sure we know what we're agreeing to and why. Because you're going to be living with this plan for a long time.*

TWENTY-FIVE

The Pessimist / Resister

---

*B*efore you dismiss the pessimists and resisters as problem participants, understand they have a gift: they see what won't work. Knowing what doesn't work is sometimes the bigger part of solving a problem.

Often the pessimist is the canary in the coal mine. Others have become oblivious to their sound because it's not a nice song. It begins to sound like constant complaints or whining.

The pessimist has often been working in their field for a long time. In their mind, their experience is a fact and evidence. They don't want to waste time, energy, or morale going through another project that will fail. They show up sounding negative and can rub others the wrong way. As facilitator, it can be useful to shine the light on their gift— knowing what's wrong—because in some cases it can help us potentially solve a problem faster.

The intervention with the pessimist goes like this.

Let's say the pessimist is named Sarah. She raises her hand and says, "I can tell you now, this isn't going to work. I've been here seventeen years, and we've done things like this in the past and they just don't stick. You're wasting your time."

> *Sarah, thank you for your experience regarding what you've seen*
> *and what you know doesn't work. Let's make sure we keep*
> *that data handy as we make decisions going forward. Thanks*
> *for your help. We were discussing X, Y, Z. What do you see as*
> *solutions to these problems so that we don't repeat history?*

Asking the pessimist what *will* work can often stop them cold. Their brains don't focus on that side of the equation very often. They may pause when you ask them to consider solutions. When you see the pause, say:

> *Get Sarah some stickies. Sarah, take a minute and write down*
> *those solutions! Add your stickies to the parking lot so we can*
> *pick up your ideas when we get to "solutions" on the agenda.*
> *Thanks.*

As facilitators, it's our role to balance out their experience if we can. That means we give their views some validation by creating a win for the team. Often one win will tip the scale for that person. Good stuff does happen.

After years of sitting through hundreds of hours of terrible meetings; watching projects fail or waste away; experiencing the merry-go-round flavor-of-the-month syndrome; and watching new managers come into the organization, implement their programs and move on in two or three years, and then being required to implement what the next new boss says, we may be able to generate some empathy for the pessimist. The pessimist is an important voice on the team. They base their viewpoints on what they have experienced. It can be devastating to watch something you poured your best efforts, creativity, hopes, and skills into fall off the radar and cost millions and millions of dollars in wasted time. The pessimist reminds us all of the price that the team pays for that in morale, momentum, and creativity It's huge.

The parting shot: some people simply see the glass half empty. If they were to win the lottery they would complain about the problems of being a multimillionaire. Use your tools and the scripts, keep your energy high, and breathe. Test their willingness to contribute in a functional way, then move on. Don't waste your time trying to convince them to change. If the behavior becomes disruptive enough to impact progress over time, they may not be a good fit for the team and may need to be replaced.

TWENTY-SIX

The Dominator

*T*he dominator can show up in many forms. They may have a strong-willed personality that becomes overbearing in a meeting. Or, they may already have the solution in their mind, having already worked through the numbers and all they want to say is, "Here it is." It may be that they are overly stressed and just want to get the thing done. Regardless of the cause, the dominator comes in and attempts to take over the conversation.

When at their worst, the dominator may huff and puff and roll their eyes when another team member raises an idea. They may come back with, "Well, here's why that won't work. Let me tell you about this. Here's the data I have." So, they interchange roles and become the know-it-all as well as the dominator. They can also be the dominator and the storyteller and the bully, all whirled into one perfect storm.

I've seen dominators come into meetings with spreadsheets and a PowerPoint they stayed up all night finishing. They've defined the problem, and it looks technical and well done. Hard to argue with the validity, or at least the veracity, of their commitment then.

"I can save us some time here. I put together the numbers and here's our path forward. Here's the problem defined. Here are the steps, and you can see this spreadsheet where I've compiled all the data. Who would take on each of these areas as a sub team? We could begin to discuss X, Y, Z..."

The dominator has had their own meeting with themselves and taken care of everything. And that's where you, as facilitator, come in.

> *Well, thank you. I appreciate all the time and energy you've put into this. And, as facilitator, my understanding of our objective is to have a fully integrated team working on this idea before we choose a path forward. So, let's put your data here as a resource for our discussion, continue with the planned agenda and hear from all the subject-matter experts. How does that sound to everyone?*

This is a scenario where having done the prework is critical. And if the dominator happens to also be the boss? This is where prework is essential for creating clear expectations, roles, and a level playing field. If the meeting is designed to ensure everyone on the team participates and weighs in on making the decision, then the dominator's approach is not going to work. However, if the prework clarified that the team's role is that of an advisory board that weighs in with questions and ideas for the boss when the proposal is presented, a completely different approach is required. In one meeting, the behavior is dysfunctional. In the other, presenting a plan is right on target. By doing thorough prework you'll know the session objective on the bull's-eye and what path to take.

If the dominator's behavior escalates and you decide to address them privately, here's a script that can support you. In this scenario we will assume this dominator is also the boss.

> *Hi, I wanted to check in with you. How are you seeing things going?*

"Well I'm not sure we're getting anywhere fast here."

> *Tell me more.*

"People are resisting my ideas. I can save us a lot of time. They don't know what I know. We can talk and talk and then they'll realize I'm right, and I just don't want to spend that time waiting for them to catch up."

> *Yeah, I hear you. Hard to be tapping your toe, waiting. I know you're super busy. And from what I remember in the prework, we discussed the benefit of getting a lot of perspectives and ideas, a big view, before making decisions. That's the phase we're in now. Is there new information the team doesn't know that you do?*

"No, it's just that I want us to move forward and get going."

> *Yes, understood. In my role as facilitator I want to make sure we stay on track and focused, and make sure everyone has a chance to offer their perspectives. I know people have taken time to prepare for this meeting and are anxious to share ideas. What would you see as the benefit, especially as the boss, to listening for new ideas and information and to being curious and open? The team will take their cues from you. The way you show up, how open you are, will cue them on how open they can be when sharing ideas. Make sense?*

"Yeah, yeah, I get you. So, I need to chill out right?"

> *(Big smile.) How about we test that, and see what happens in the next agenda item after break?*

"Okay."

> *Thanks for being willing.*

TWENTY-SEVEN

The Bully

*T*here are varying degrees of bullying, as with all the dysfunctional behaviors. Some bullying behaviors are overt, others are subtle.

I was in a meeting with two brothers who were on the same team. They were both high-level managers. The work of their departments overlapped, and these departments were integral to each other. Both had been in this field for many years.

Early in the meeting they started bantering. "Well, Steve knows that in order to get anything done, he has to come talk to me because he can't really come up with his own ideas. It's been like that our whole life."

Steve turned a little red. Just a little. "Uh-huh. That's my baby brother and his perfection complex."

Over the next half an hour, a couple more barbs were thrown between them. "Well, if you could get your team together and work on that, we wouldn't be having all these problems. Ha, ha, ha. But I know, I know, you guys will get it together, I know. I'm not worried about it." But the barb was already sent and hooked in.

As facilitators this is our cue to go back to the agreements.

Hey, I want to check in here. How many of you agree we want to operate at a high professional level?

(You raise your hand, other hands go up, and heads nod.)

Okay, great. And how many of you agree we don't want anything happening in here that would impact our professionalism or respect for each other?

(Raise your hand up again. Everyone will respond with another yes.)

Alright. Let's go back to the agreements, particularly "respect the speaker." I get it. A lot of you know each other outside this room. Some of you have history together. I bet you've had some great stories you could share, huh, at break?

"Yes. Ha, ha, ha."

In here, I wouldn't want anything like that—the familiarity, camaraderie—to negatively affect what we're trying to accomplish. Or, in the heat of a serious discussion, the bantering, the teasing, to cross the line. How many of you would agree we can hold this kind of teasing for your break, and in here, we'll keep our discussions totally professional? Raise our bar?

The team says, "Yes!"

Great. Thanks everybody. Okay, where were we?

Occasionally the teasing may come up again.

Back to this idea of teasing. I'm noticing that it just happened, and we're creatures of what, everybody?

Everybody says, "Habit!"

Habit. Yes. So, a friendly reminder: we're holding the teasing during our meeting so we stay on track and focused. Yes?

They say, "Yes."

Great, thank you.

If it happens again, call a break. As people file out of the room, you catch the bully, or bullies, and call them over. This will be your private level-two intervention. In this case we go into the private meeting more directly. We've already addressed the group generally two times. Everyone knows who the dysfunctional people are.

Hi, let's talk. Checking in about the teasing. It's starting to impact our work. Case in point, we're here on a break to discuss this. What's happening for you? How can I help?

"Oh gosh, you know, it's just how we operate. Everybody knows that. I don't think it's a big deal."

I can appreciate that's how you've been operating. And you have a long relationship as family. In my role as facilitator, I'm responsible for making sure we're operating under the agreements and keeping the meeting on track. I'm wondering what you're willing to do to stop the teasing and the banter while you're in this meeting?

"Hey, sorry, we can stop. Just stick to work stuff."

Great I appreciate that. I think we can get some really good work done in here today. Thanks. See you after break.

TWENTY-EIGHT

The Wallflower

---

*E*xpect to facilitate meetings where some people simply do not engage. They won't say anything, they won't put their hands up, they won't ask questions. What's happening? What to do? What if it's the boss?

Here are some of the reasons people don't engage:

- Introverted or shy
- Not feeling well
- Underdeveloped social skills
- Personal issues outside of work
- Conflict with team members (personal and/or professional)
- Afraid to speak in public
- Unprepared
- Beaten down or embarrassed in other meetings
- Don't know why they're in this meeting (not sure how to participate)
- Tired
- Don't want the session objective to be reached because it will potentially impact them negatively
- They don't like you

- Used to being told what to do and don't have the skills to participate (see "afraid to speak in public")

What do you do if you're facilitating a meeting and there's at least one wallflower? Here's the good news: no matter the root cause of their behavior—any behavior—the intervention is the same.

Let's assume that the prework is done and you have the right people in the room. And still, there is someone who won't engage. Do a check in. First, make sure that they're aware of and clear about their role. They're in the meeting as a subject-matter expert on the topic of X, and here's how that fits into accomplishing the session objective. Help them see how the dots connect and why they're a part of this meeting.

You will have already covered this in the prework, and will cover it again when you open the session (you'll find the script for opening the session in the next section: Mechanics of a Great Meeting).

> That's why you're all here. As subject-matter experts, each of you
> plays an important role. We're looking for your experience
> and ideas as a resource so that we can accomplish this session
> objective.

Now you begin the meeting. Sometimes the wallflower is tracking the discussion and looks engaged, but just isn't speaking.

What personality and work-style assessments tell us is that for more logic-driven (left-brain) thinkers, decision-making takes more time. Processing information, analyzing it, and coming to a conclusion in order to make a solid decision isn't a quick or reactive process. Their silence is not an indication something is going wrong. They may be processing the information they're hearing and don't have anything to contribute yet. This is another reason the prework is so important: the wallflower has time to prepare, research, ponder, and get ready to ask questions before the meeting.

That's why we build in small group sharing processes throughout the meeting to warm people up and set a comfortable context. This way, if the wallflower doesn't speak in a large group setting they have the opportunity to contribute in the small group, and typically they will.

While you have probably seen or heard of this approach for getting the wallflower to speak up, in my experience, calling on someone who isn't speaking doesn't work. Don't put them on the spot. Their nonverbal communication is screaming out, "I'm not ready to speak up yet!" Because if they were comfortable, they would already be speaking. It tends to close them down even further rather than opening them up. And we know that for many people, speaking in front of others is a top fear.

Here are some other ideas.

Level 1: Address the Group Generally

Engage the power of proximity and walk into the U. Open your arms up wide, and smile.

> *For those of you who have been listening to this conversation, tracking it, what are you hearing? What are we missing? What parts are standing out for you? I would love to hear from everybody through your lenses as subject-matter experts. What do you see from the finance, engineering and human resources perspective?*

Level 2: Take a Break and Talk Privately

If the wallflower still doesn't speak up after being prompted, it's time to move to level-two intervention, which involves taking a break and talking to them privately. Use the script from Chapter 22 (Address Dysfunction).

> *Hey, how's it going? What are you seeing happening in the meeting? What are you seeing through your perspective? I'd*

love to hear from you. We really could use your perspective.
What can I do to help with that?

Engage your empathy. How do you get them in the game? How do you get them warmed up? How do you get them off the bench and onto the field?

On the first day of a thirty-five-person, three-day strategic planning session, one of the key members of the leadership team hadn't spoken all morning. After the second break two team members came over to me and said, "Hey we'd love to hear from Rose, she's our boss. Wondering why she's not weighing in?"

I found Rose toward the end of the break.

Hi, how do you see things going so far?

"Great," Rose said.

Hey, your team would love to hear from you.

"Really? Geez, I wanted to keep my mouth shut and give them some space to talk!"

Well, feel free to jump in. I think they're looking forward to
hearing your ideas as well.

After break Rose did jump right in. Because of the good relationship she had with her team, she was able to encourage them to participate in the larger group by saying things like, "Here's what I've been seeing. This is really Litza's wheelhouse. She did the majority of the work and is the expert in this area." Beautiful. Rose didn't call on Litza to speak, yet still gave her credit, acknowledged her expertise, showed respect for her work, and gave her an opening to jump in. A great example of leadership.

If the silent person gets called out by another co-worker, intervene and support!

> *Jennie, what are you seeing from your perspective as the subject*
> *matter expert in finance?*

If Jennie freezes, you jump in.

> *Hey, how about some sticky notes? Let's get Jennie that pad and*
> *marker. Jennie, give yourself a moment to jot down what's*
> *coming to mind and we'll get back to you in a bit. Okay*
> *everybody, who else has ideas about this?*

Remember, we don't need to spend time in our own heads trying to figure out what's causing others' dysfunction. Because we're really only guessing. It's a lot faster to call a break and ask the person directly.

How and what you ask them are key when you're addressing dysfunction. And it's all about asking open-ended questions beginning with the words *what, how,* and *why.*

I've seen facilitators waste a lot of time asking closed-ended questions like these:

"So, Jennie, are you afraid? Is it because Bill is in the room and he's your boss? Is it because of that other meeting?"

And Jennie is saying, "No, no, no."

Save time and energy. Cut to the chase and *ask* rather than guess.

> *How's the meeting going for you? I'm noticing you haven't*
> *weighed in yet. How can I help?*

Then listen. You'll get your correct answer much faster. No need to spend time wondering, "Do they feel this way?" or, "Are they thinking this?" Watch out for wanting to diagnose somebody. You're not a mind reader.

TWENTY-NINE

Mission Control

---

*I*t's not uncommon for teams to be assigned to a project that was initiated far up the chain of command. At the local level, the project feels like an awkward or even impossible fit. Teams are confused and turned off by the objective, and they might be resistant, pessimistic, and disheartened. However, the decision has been made and the team is going forward.

Rallying this team can be difficult. They're clear about what they 'can't' do, and that's all they can see. Their brains and their energy shut down. They feel powerless and stuck. I've used the mission-control exercise with teams in this situation—teams who feel like conditions are out of their control. It empowers them to shift their thinking, see new possibilities and find ways around obstacles that used to stop them.

It reveals the perceptions and biases around what a team can control—and what they can't. There is almost always more in their control than they realize. Often the genesis of the initial resistance can be traced back to how the meeting was set up, in case you needed another reminder about the importance of solid prework.

Using Mission Control

There are two ways to use mission control. The first is as an intervention, when we detect during the session that the team is feeling deflated and continuing with the agenda is not going to produce the results needed. And the second is as a specific agenda item to use with a team that you believe might need a little confidence boost regarding their ability to achieve the objectives. You may already see signs of pessimism on this team. Or, because of the nature of the project, you simply know they will benefit from seeing how much they can still control even when it may appear that external (read: bosses higher up) forces are pulling all the strings.

Here's an introduction and script for the unplanned mission-control exercise with a team that exhibits signs of feeling deflated while in the midst of a session.

How is everybody doing?

They're flat.

What do we need to talk about that might not be on the agenda?
It feels like there might be something...

They may respond that they don't want to do this, that they don't want to be in this position.

Okay, got it. How much control do we have over that?

Let them weigh in.

Okay then. What I'm hearing is that we don't have control over
whether we do this or not?

Right.

What we do have control over is how we will do this thing?
Would that be true?

Right.

So how would you like this to go? How can we turn this lemon
into lemonade? We can set this up as you saw in the prework
email, to be fast and efficient, etcetera. Part of that is on me.
A bigger part is on whom?

Us.

Yes. Who has the power to decide how it goes?

We do.

Let's take a look at what's in our control and what's not. We
focus on what we can do and not on the stuff we can't do
anything about.

Here's the script for introducing a preplanned use of the exercise.

Okay team our next agenda item is called "mission control." Ever
notice how we can focus a lot of time, energy, and discussion
on things we have no control over? Things we won't be able to
change? Like whether or not we have a say about doing this
project? Let's use that energy to look at what we do have
control over and leveraging our resources there. How's that
sound? This will be fun.

And, whether unplanned or planned, here's the script for the
mission-control exercise.

The supplies you'll need are markers, sticky notes, and two easel
stands with chart pads, or two sheets of chart paper taped on a wall
side by side. You'll want one set for each small team.

Let's take a few moments to clarify where we want to focus in our
project: where we can influence, what we can influence, and
how we can make a difference when we're able. That will save
us lots of time and energy.

Next, you'll next divide the teams into small groups. Assemble those small groups in chairs in a horseshoe layout at an easel station or in front of a wall chart. Ask for volunteers to be the recorder.

Instructions for the recorder:

Thanks for being the recorder. Here are a few instructions. You'll
be writing down your team's ideas on the sticky notes. One
idea per sticky note. Write big. Think "bullet point" and leave
out "and", "but", and "the". Remember to get your own ideas
in there, too.

This is a brainstorm session. No need to discuss, agree, or disagree
with ideas. As many ideas as possible is what we're looking
for in this step. This is a speed exercise. Recorders ready?
Questions?

Here's the question you're working on: thinking about our
project, the scope, budget, timing, resources, (fill in the blank)
make a list of all of the things that aren't in our control. I'll
set the timer for two minutes. Go!

Teams make their sticky-note list for two minutes. When the two minutes are up, have each recorder put the sticky notes up on the chart. Ask the recorder to add a title to the chart:

NOT in Our Control

Now it's time for the debrief. Each small team reads their list.

> *How does spending time and energy on the things on this "not in*
> *our control" list impact your work?*
> *Why do you think we spend time focused on the items on this list?*

Now for the next round.

> *Thinking about the project again, the scope, budget, timing,*
> *resources—what is in our control?*

Teams make their sticky-note lists for two minutes. Once again, ask
the recorder to put the sticky notes up on the chart. This time they'll
title the chart:

IN Our Control

For the debrief, each team reports on their list.

> *Let's look at the "in our control" list. What can we focus on in*
> *this list to help us as we go forward?*

Typically, there are many sticky notes on the "NOT" sheet and only
a few on the "IN" sheet.

> *Now imagine, with our best creative thinking—what could we do*
> *to move some "NOT" items into the "IN" list? Which ones*
> *might move? What would it take to make them move, to make*
> *that happen?*

Let the teams work and discuss how to move items. Check in with
them after ten minutes.

> *How's everybody doing? Who would like more time?*

Give them a couple more minutes if needed.
Small groups report out round robin. They listen for strategies for

how to move "NOT in our control" items to the "IN our control" chart.

For the next round, ask the large group to discuss and share ideas to support the small teams in determining how to move items remaining on the "NOT" sheet over to the "IN" sheet.

The magic in this exercise is in watching the team's energy and creativity shift as they begin to see ways around obstacles as they move stickies from "NOT" to "IN".

When one "NOT" sticky moves, another "NOT" is affected, and a solution becomes obvious where one wasn't seen before. Often, at the end of this exercise, the "NOT in our control" sheet is left with only one or two stickies and the "IN our control" sheet is stuffed full. Beautiful!

> *Great work, team! Looking at where we started and where we are*
> *now, what did you learn in this exercise? How can we use this*
> *information as we move forward? Give your neighbor a high*
> *five and tell them, "You're awesome!"*

And that's it. Mission control will almost always help you clear a team logjam, reenergize discussions and move the team forward with a renewed sense of empowerment and, best of all, hope. Try this exercise yourself when you feel stuck. It's frequently shown me the way when I've been lost in turbulent water.

Section VI: Mechanics of a Great Meeting

THIRTY

Prep and Room Setup

*Y*our prep and room setup are directly linked to your prework. Yup. We're back to where we started. Prework is critical for more than the objective setting, team selection, sales and marketing, interviews, and invitation emails. It also involves planning exactly how you'll set up the room, based on the agenda, and planning the group processes the team will be involved in to gather and share information to achieve your session objective.

As you plan your room setup, you'll want to consider how many people are attending. Will a U-shaped setup be possible? As I've mentioned, the U shape can accommodate up to thirty people and is my favorite room-setup style. It makes it easier for you to facilitate the meeting, makes it easier for participants to engage, and helps level the playing field if there are hierarchical rankings at play. If you have more than thirty people and you want small teams or a more intimate setup for small groups, you'll want to switch to small-table groups.

Regardless of whether you end up in a U shape or at tables, it's a good idea to plan how you'll break a larger group into smaller groups from the start of the meeting. Smaller groups help people warm up in a meeting. They also do the following:

- Give everyone a chance to speak up. People who are less

comfortable talking in a large group tend to contribute more in a small group.
- Help people warm up, resulting in team members who stay more engaged (participation and energy both go up!).
- Result in more ideas and creative, innovative thinking.

How to Break a Big Team into Small Ones

Get the team roster. Divide the team members into groups of four to five. A team of twenty means five groups of four, or four groups of five, etcetera. It's easy to do with name tents, which I'll get to in a moment.

Depending on your session objective and agenda, you may want to break up departments and create cross-functional teams. In some cases, it may be a benefit to have small teams that keep functional groups together: finance with finance, engineering with engineering. Don't overthink this. Keep it simple. You can always reshuffle for the next meeting, or in the afternoon of an all-day session.

Making Name Tents

Think back to meetings you've been in. You arrive, walk into the room and figure out where to sit. You look around to see who else is there, and where the coffee is. You're getting settled in, putting your things down. You greet the person next to you. They tell you their name, and two seconds later you can't remember it. Yup, this happens all the time.

The fix is the name tent. You'll write names on both sides of the name tent. Most of us are visual learners, meaning when we can see something, we can file it and remember the data for a longer time. People next to each other can more easily remember each other's names if they can easily glance over the tents and remind themselves.

Use heavy card stock folded in half length-wise so you have a long rectangle. Each small team gets a color. Write names on the tents using a felt marker in the team color. Make a name tent for yourself, too, using a totally different color. Why? It only took a couple of participants early on in my career saying, "I see you like the red (or the blue) team best!" when I used a team's color for my name tent. People pay attention. And some people want to stir the pot. Make it easy and stay neutral.

Red: Litza, Tim, Mike S., and Ava
Blue: Lindsey, Jack, Brad, and Kristine
Green: Liz, Sam, Juan, Annie
Purple: David, Kelly, Rose, Ahmed
Orange: Karen, William, Aaron, Shelley

Sticky Notes

Place a three-by-five-inch sticky-note pad and marker in the team's color on the table in front of each small team. You'll be able to track ideas from each team as they begin to do their work. Purple team ideas are written in purple, green team ideas are written in green, etcetera. Simple and very effective.

Small Group Work

How you plan your small group work will impact your agenda. Mixing up large and small group work has a number of advantages: it mixes up the energy and allows people to warm up socially in a smaller group, which greases the wheel for contributions in the larger group setting. Plan for intermittent small group work right from the start.

As you open the session, ask the small teams to put their heads together and gather ideas about what they want to get out of the session. A designated recorder writes each idea on a separate sticky note. Then each team reports out around the room as you put their sticky notes on the easel. You will see themes emerge. Great minds think alike!

To keep the energy and engagement up, it helps to keep mixing up your approach. For the second agenda item, consider having participants work with partners. A team of five or six can be broken into two teams of three and three, or two and three, to brainstorm and discuss ideas. For the third agenda item, go back to small teams, and for the fourth engage in a whole-group discussion. With everyone warmed up more people will participate in the large group. If you don't incorporate small group work at the beginning, personalities can begin to dominate early. Others shut down and/or let the high-energy contributors do the work.

Agenda Timing

Be mindful that getting small groups set up to record their ideas, gather them, and then discuss them in a large group takes time. And it's definitely worth your effort! Let's use an example of a team of twenty and look at how long it might take to cover one agenda item.

- Five minutes for set up instructions and questions.
- Ten to twenty minutes in small group discussion.
- Ten minutes to collect, read, and post sticky notes.
- Fifteen to twenty minutes, depending on the objective of the agenda item, for discussion as a large group.

It can easily take one hour to get through a relatively straight-forward agenda item. Give yourself flexibility, and whatever you do, don't post times on the agenda you circulate to the team in the introduction and welcome email, or in the agenda you post on a chart at the front of the room. Of course, you will have your working agenda timed to the minute—the team doesn't need to see those details. In fact, they can become distracting for them.

Caution: Don't Overload Your Agenda

It is really easy and really common to *overload your agenda*. Don't be afraid to leave yourself some wiggle room, an extra ten to fifteen minutes sprinkled into the agenda in the morning and again in the afternoon.

For a one-hour meeting, plan for a forty-five-minute agenda. If we don't complete all the agenda items, it looks as if we failed, or as if we didn't get done what we set out to do. And people who were prepared to speak to a particular agenda item don't get their chance. We may be tempted to let the meeting run late and hold people hostage. Some facilitators may want to blame the team, when in reality the agenda was unrealistic for what could be accomplished in that time slot.

You might think you'll save time by having only large group discussions. Yes, logically that's true. It can be faster to move through items with the large group. However, you will lose out on the increased participation, idea generation, and teamwork that is developed through small group work.

[For a complete pre-meeting set up checklist, visit http://www.superteams.com.]

THIRTY-ONE

Opening the Session

There are three main parts to opening the session. They act as a bridge between the prework that you were able to do and what the team will see when they walk into the meeting room.

Here are the three parts:

1. The setup
2. The kick-off
3. Showtime!

In the next few chapters we'll break each of those parts down.

The Setup

If you're not familiar with the meeting location or the room, visit the site and the room a few days or a week before the meeting. As you look around, ask yourself these questions:

- What do I need to bring?
- What are some of the challenges going to be?
- How do I log in on the computer in that room?
- How does the sound system work?

- Do I need keys to get into the room?
- Do I need an escort to get into the room?
- What paperwork might be required to access the location?
- Do I need keys to get into the supply room inside the meeting room?
- Can I post paper on the wall? What is my plan if I can't?

The more you know before the meeting starts, the fewer the surprises. The fewer the surprises, the more relaxed and in control you're going to look and feel.

Arrive at least thirty to sixty minutes ahead of the start time. Give yourself enough time to get the room set up the way you want. And have it all done and handled before people start coming in. You don't want to look or feel rushed. This is especially important if it's a first meeting with a new team, or a big kick-off meeting for a new project. You likely have a little more leeway on your early arrival if this is a weekly department meeting in a room you're familiar with. Use your best judgment. If you're not sure, err on the side of arriving earlier.

Back-to-back Meetings

What about the back-to-back meetings scenario, where you and your team are waiting at the conference room door for another meeting to wrap up before you can get in to set up for your 10:00 a.m. meeting? You're going to make lemonade out of that lemon. This is where your planning and prework will serve you, big time.

Knock on the door. You'll hear people gathering their gear, pushing chairs back and standing up. Your team files in. Typically, both teams will chat a bit as they pass. Your team is seated by 10:06 a.m., and your 10:00 meeting really gets started at 10:10. At 10:53 someone from the meeting scheduled to happen in this same room at 11:00 opens the door: "Oops!" This is enough of an inadvertent interruption to push your team into "almost time to leave" mode. They start to gather their things while you're trying to wrap up the last agenda item —and you haven't even had time to review the parking lot. Your sixty-minute meeting turns out to be only forty minutes of actual work time, if you're lucky to get that much.

Meetings happen like this constantly—scheduled back to back with no consideration of the efficiency impact. It's a huge time and dollar waster. And a blind spot.

What can you do? I've worked with teams using this solution with great results. Test it with your teams and see how it works.

Look at the meeting room schedule. Who is going to be in the room before you? Contact the leader/facilitator. In person is best.

> *Hi, I see you're booked in ahead of me in Room A for next*
> *Tuesday. I've got an idea about saving both of us some time*
> *Do you have a minute?*

"Of course." (Who wouldn't jump at the chance to save some time?)

> *How would it work for you if I corralled my team and kept them*
> *away from the door, so you aren't interrupted. I'll be clear*
> *with my team that they are to arrive at 10:05. I'll start our*
> *meeting at 10:10. That will give your team plenty of time to*
> *be out by 10:00, and I'll have enough cushion to set up and*
> *get my team in.*

I guarantee you they'll say yes. Then contact the person who will be coming in after you.

> *I have an idea. I'm looking at ways to save us time shuffling*
> *between meetings. How would it work for you if I make sure*
> *we're out of the room by 10:55? And you let your team know*
> *not to show until 11:00? We'll be sure to have the room clear*
> *and ready for you to go in and get started?*

But wait! I know what you're thinking. You're thinking that you will have just talked yourself into a forty-five-minute meeting when it was supposed to be an hour, right? Right. In this case, I have a higher purpose in mind. What you're doing in this scenario is starting the habit of paying attention to meeting start and end times *within the organization*. And it's contagious. You'll be raising the bar for expectations and increasing performance in your own meetings as well as in the meetings of other people. Simply by drawing attention to the concept of starting and ending on time. Some teams work with this approach better than others, but overall, the benefits of these seemingly small things add up. It's worth it.

Here's the result I've seen using this approach. My team is briefed on why this will increase our actual work time in the meeting. We're in the room at 10:10, and then we work with a sense of focus and urgency that moves the discussions along. A solid focused forty minutes. We get a lot done. At 10:50, we wrap up, and we're out of the room at 10:55.

Expect Lemons—Make Lemonade

Even with solid prework and planning, the unexpected is going to happen. Let's say you show up to facilitate a multi-day training session, and you've confirmed ahead of time with your point person that the room will be set up in a U-shape. You absolutely checked and double-checked. You show up expecting to find your five easels set up with chart pads in front of the U... only to find the room set up in classroom style. No easels or chart pads in sight. And you haven't been able to get into the building until now—twenty minutes before the training session is to start. Aaak!

So, there you are, hustling, moving furniture, sweating, asking people to find the key to the supply closet so you can get the easels and chart pads out. You're going to make lemonade out of that lemon, too. Because you've done your prework and planning, you've set yourself up to better handle situations like these, when you don't have the time you'd like. You do the set up in accelerated mode. And because you've planned, you know exactly what to do.

What happens when you show up and you can't get in? At all? Or, when you show up and they've got you in the wrong room? You might want to curse and swear (under your breath, of course!). What do you do?

Take a deep breath and decide. React or respond? You choose: how will I *be* about this? What kind of leader do I want to show up as? People are watching. What will I model when the heat gets turned up? I am responsible for the energy I bring into the room.

In your mind you're saying, "What the ...? Where was the miss here? We confirmed and re-confirmed." At that moment finding the root cause of the issue is not the priority. That will come after the meeting. For now? You do the very best you can. Expect lemons. How will you make lemonade, really good-tasting lemonade, out of this? Here's what you'll do. Bring the sugar! You'll find a couple of people who are willing to help, and you'll get it done. And it's for this scenario that you want to be organized walking into opening a session. So that when (not if) the unexpected happens you're as prepared as you can be. You've got all of the other things handled already. You won't freak out. You'll set up your music, shift the energy around, and set the tone you want. And, of course, you'll start on time.

Check Your Supplies

In your prework, you decided how you're going to handle each agenda item. What supplies do you need to set up for each?

- **Chart stands** (easels) and **chart pads**. Two for you and one for each small group. If the meeting room doesn't have its own easels and chart pads, bring your own. Another option if you don't have easels: record ideas on sticky notes and post them directly on the wall. Or, try the easel size self-sticking chart pads— post the paper right on the wall and work from there. Put several sheets up in case your markers bleed through the paper! Leaving marker on wallpaper doesn't always get you asked back. Just sayin'. Oops.
- **Masking tape.** Pre-tear it and place it on the back of the

chart stand. What's your wall plan for hanging charts as they're recorded? Please see my website, www.superteams.com, for a checklist of alternative ideas in case you cannot tape material to the walls.

- **Markers, pens, paper.** Make sure you bring along a good, juicy, brand-new set of markers in assorted colors even if your on-site contact person says, "Oh, we'll have markers there, don't you worry." The ones your contact brings might be dry-erase markers, and you're using paper. Or, the caps might have been left off or something.

- **Timer.** Have some sort of timer device, whether it's on your phone or you bring a dedicated standalone timer.

- **Sticky notes.** Lots of sticky notes. One pad for each small team and the corresponding color marker. I like the three-by-five size, as they're small enough for a single idea and big enough that they can be seen when they're stuck up on the chart at the front of the room. Put these on the tables around the room.

- **Play-Doh.** For those who learn by doing (kinesthetic learning style) and may have trouble sitting still through the discussion. Put out small individual tubs for each participant when you are setting up. When you're opening the session, let them know it's theirs to use. Your script: *The Play-doh is for you to use. Sometimes it's nice to have something to do with your hands when you're sitting.* That's all you have to say. It's incredible what people will create!

- **Name tents.** Use the colored markers on the name tents to divide the large group into small groups for breakout work.

- **The five pillars and premade charts.** Session objective, agenda, agreements, decision-making method and parking lot.

- **Your music.**

- **Water.** And treats for yourself.

This is the nitty gritty toolbox stuff that can easily get overlooked. And if you don't have this stuff?

You won't easily be able to set expectations or remind people about agreements.

You'll have no mechanism to divert the dominator or the storyteller.

Your meeting will suck.

Check Your AV Equipment

Someone is going to come up to you, or call you, the day before the meeting and say, "Hey, I'm going to send you my PowerPoint presentation. Would you log in and get it all set up for me tomorrow morning?"

Um, the answer is no.

> *Oh, sorry. No. I wish I could. How about this. Meet me there thirty minutes before the meeting is slated to start. I'll pour you a cup of coffee, and you can get yourself logged in, so you won't have any trouble with that.*

As it gets closer to meeting time, especially if there are going to be presentations, the last-minute people will be scrambling to get their stuff done. And then they'll want you to have it up and ready for them. You just don't have time for that. It's okay to say no.

Introduce Yourself

As people arrive, shake their hands and say hi. Keep your psychic muscles in shape and check on how the room is feeling as people file in. Your energy when you welcome folks to the meeting helps set the tone for the session. Smile, warm up the group, discuss neutral topics such as sports and the weather.

This is one of the reasons why you want to be set up with time to spare—so you can welcome people when they arrive. Think of it like hosting a party. You're also running interference in case anybody shows up at the meeting and immediately wants to start talking about some of the problems or issues. It doesn't take long for people to start getting into cliques and all lathered up before the meeting. Someone might be pissed off and walk in with their own agenda, ready to vent at the group. Make sure your radar is on and that you break up that kind of stuff by going over and talking about the weather, parking, what they had for breakfast, or good places to get coffee. Nice tie, shoes, hat... Where did you go on vacation? All these topics are fair game.

Just don't start the meeting before the meeting starts.

THIRTY-TWO

Kick-off

_____

*N*ow you're ready to go live! Bring your biggest and best self forward so you look and act as if you're at the top of the food chain. Establish yourself as the alpha in the room. Own it. I call this centering and anchoring.

Remember when we talked about predatory behavior and animals that hunt in packs? (See Chapter 3.) They're looking for the weak one. Looking and sounding weak triggers people to act differently. Using statements such as, "I don't like being up in front of people," or, "I've never done this before—I hope you'll cut me some slack," sets the facilitator up to look like a wounded gazelle. Like food. This subconsciously gives the team permission to behave like a pack of hyenas that haven't eaten in three weeks. They don't want to waste their time in a meeting with a facilitator who doesn't know what they're doing.

Even if you've never facilitated before, don't say that out loud. I'm sure we've all been in a meeting where somebody tried to knock the facilitator off of the front of the room, right? It's not pretty. When you establish yourself as the alpha in the room you're helping ensure it doesn't happen to you. The power of the opening-the-session script, when you rehearse it and stick to it, is that in using it, you cannot fail.

Winging It

I don't care who you are, how senior you are, or how many meetings you've opened or sessions you've facilitated. If you're winging it, everybody can tell. You're not doing anyone any favors. You can't hide when you're at the front of the room. You can't fake prepared.

I've seen facilitators who haven't given the meeting a thought, and they say that out loud in front of the team as a way to garner sympathy for their unpreparedness. "Gosh, I'm *so* busy. What do we want to talk about today?" Ugh. They've just set the bar for performance, and it's a low one. And now they're holding their team hostage in a meeting that sucks.

Facilitator Persona

As facilitators, we're human too. Some days are better than others. Some days we could really use some extra help to ramp up our energy and bring our A game. I've known facilitators who almost take on another personality when they're at the front of the room. Like Clark Kent changing into Superman. There are some people who need to do that. It may be that they realize facilitating or standing up in front of a group takes them beyond their comfort zone. This isn't a bad thing as long as you can maintain your authenticity. Whatever works for you. If you're not a smiler, or you don't want to speak up in a voice that can project to the back of the meeting room, that's fine—as a participant. However, if you're in the leadership/facilitator role, and you want the team to get results, smiling and projecting your voice and bringing more energy to the room are core tools to master.

My facilitator training sessions are hands-on and interactive. Participants watch their teammates using the tools, interacting, getting feedback, fine tuning, working it again, and seeing their own improvement. They find out just how easy it is to facilitate when they have a chance to practice with reliable tools and skills. Sometimes taking on a facilitator super hero persona can help them get out of their head and have fun with it.

Here's a secret. I have two facilitator super hero personas: Madonna and Mother Theresa. When I need to crack the whip, Madonna's approach is suitable. In other situations, where more empathy is called for, it takes a touch of Mother Theresa.

Many people still don't realize that meetings can be fun, engaging, and energizing, and the bonus is that you get work done, too! Having a little fun with your team is a great creativity opener for the brain. Who can you channel as your facilitator super hero? How would they show up in the front of the room?

Kickoff and the Two-Minute Warning

Two minutes before the meeting is officially set to begin, you'll give the team a heads up that the meeting will start in two minutes. Use a welcoming tone. It's an invitation, not a demand. Smile.

> *Good morning everybody! This is your two-minute warning. We'll be starting in two minutes. Now is a good time to finish up what you're doing, power down electronics, and get something to drink. We'll start in two minutes.*

Then you'll set your timer for two minutes and get ready to begin.

The Timer

I use the timer on my phone, but a little kitchen timer works too. The idea is to use the timing device of your choosing to keep yourself and the team on track. The team quickly gets used to hearing the auditory signal. It's the same with the music. The music becomes a timing device as well. You shut the music off and people know break is done. And they come back in from the halls.

How to Use Your Two Minutes

In those two minutes, between the warning and when the timer goes off, get yourself ready to go live. Your ability to deliver a solid, well-prepared opening sets the tone for the meeting and establishes your facilitator credibility.

- Anchor yourself. Feel your feet in your shoes.
- Take a deep slow breath in, then out. Repeat.
- Scan the audience.
- Look over your opening script.
- Use bullet points as cues for your notes vs. reading from the paper.
- Don't use slides for the opening.

As you get ready to go live during the two-minute warning, it's normal to experience a range of emotions. You may feel excited, anxious, or even scared. While you take a couple of deep breaths to center yourself, look over your showtime script to get the first few steps set in your mind. Using the script will keep you on track and looking prepared and organized.

Body Language

You want to be sure that your body language, gestures and facial expressions match what you're saying. Be sure your audio matches your video. And it doesn't for a lot of leaders. They're saying one thing and doing another. Here are some tips to help focus your attention on the right kind of body language.

- Think "warm and friendly."
- Face the audience.
- Smile—people will smile back.
- Stand up tall.
- Project your voice, vary your tone.

THIRTY-THREE

Showtime

---

*O*nce your two-minute timer goes off, shut off the music. It's *showtime.* You begin the opening-the-session script—right on time—no matter what. No matter who is in the room. Or who isn't.

Alright everyone. Take your seat. Let's get started.

Your energy is high. You're smiling, excited, and confident. Even if a few stragglers are getting back to their seats with coffee, you start.

Stick to the Script

The script describes the five pillars, including the meeting process and how you and your team will work together. The order of the script works like a winning game of dominoes. Each step falls effortlessly into the next step.

Why Use a Script?

One of the great benefits of the script is that all the "hook" words are removed. Hook words are things we say that may trigger dysfunction. For example, you may be familiar with the term "ground rules".

Ground rules are often used as a way to manage behavior during a meeting.

At the beginning of a meeting, when people are anywhere from curious to skeptical, talking about rules as you're determining how the meeting is going to go can imply that you view this team and their anticipated behavior as problematic and unruly. It sets up an adversarial, us-versus-them environment.

In our sessions we change "ground rules" to "agreements," which are ways we agree to work together in the meeting. The agreements reflect that. They ask for what we want, not for what we don't want. For example: "respect the speaker" rather than "no interrupting."

Another common ground rule you may hear is, "there are no stupid ideas." Meaning, no idea is stupid so please speak up and say what's on your mind. However, the little voice in most people's heads will say in response, "Oh, yes there are stupid ideas, and I've heard them…" Using the words "no stupid ideas" begins to unconsciously change behavior; rather than opening up participation, it closes people down.

Change "no stupid ideas" to "all ideas welcome."

Upgrading from "ground rules" to "agreements" is step one. Your step two is to go over each agreement out loud with the team. By doing so, you're setting the context and preventing dysfunction. This is time well spent with a new team or as you begin using these tools with your existing team. The script gives you the words to describe each agreement, so you don't have to assume everyone agrees on the definition. Assuming is risky. One person's definition of "respect" can be very different from a teammate's definition of the same word. Close the gap and take the time to cover each agreement in detail.

I've heard many a facilitator/leader say, while looking at a chart or PowerPoint slide, "And these will be our ground rules. OK? Anybody got any questions on those?" Everyone habitually shakes their heads, indicating they're on board. The facilitator doesn't go over them. If you don't cover what each one means and get the team's buy-in, it's difficult to refer to the agreements later in a level one intervention. The dysfunctional person can come right back with, "Well I didn't know you meant *that!* I didn't know 'respect the speaker' meant no whispering!"

As the facilitator your job is to stick to the script. Rehearse and memorize it so when you're up front, and perhaps a bit nervous, you're solid on what comes out of your mouth. You are now the focal point of the whole room. Remember: when your emotions go up, your intelligence goes down. If you can't remember what to say, the script will be there to rescue you!

THIRTY-FOUR

The Showtime Script

*W*hy is opening the session—and how you open it—important? Because it sets the tone for the whole meeting. Using a script will help keep you as facilitator on track and focused. The script is a repeatable and effective framework that saves you time, steers you clear of missteps and enhances both your reputation and the team's performance.

Ideally, you will have already had a chance to meet with each member of the team during the interviews in the prework. In your "welcome to the team" email, the session objective, the first meeting agenda, the agreements, the decision-making method, and the parking lot will already have been introduced. When the team walks into the room and sees the charts on the wall it won't be a surprise. An environment with no surprises leads to a decrease in anxiety and an increase in the comfort level overall. The more relaxed the team feels, the easier it is for them to get into doing quality work. In the cases where you don't have the option to do the prework interviews, using these "showtime" steps will increase success in defining boundaries and expectations for an effective and efficient session.

Here's the entire showtime script. Everything in *italics* is what you say out loud to the team. Remember to smile, make eye contact, and set your energy high.

Two HMOY Questions

The script begins with two "how many of you" questions, which I abbreviate to HMOY. The HMOY questions are designed to get the team engaged, and focused, and to begin the process of setting the bar high for participation. The session objective informs the HMOY questions you create in your prework and the tone in which you'll ask them. Pump up the energy if it's appropriate for what's being discussed. Create your HMOY questions so they can be answered with a yes. And, of course your hand is raised high as you ask your HMOY questions.

Let's imagine your session objective is to improve the hiring process. Your HMOY questions could sound like this:

> *How many of you have ever thought the hiring process could be*
> *made even better?*
> *How many of you would like to get going and get that done?*

For a weekly department meeting:

> *HMOY would like to move the ball forward on our big goals?*
> *How about we get to work and make that happen?*

Your hand is up, their hands are up.

> *Great, you've come to the right place.*

Your Name

You don't need to introduce yourself if this is a weekly meeting and you know everyone well. Otherwise...

> *My name is _____.*

Acknowledgment and Thanks

HMOY could be doing something else with your time today?
  Thank you for taking your time and energy to be here today.
  You have my promise I'll do everything in my power to make
  sure your time is well spent.

WIIFM—What's In It for Me?

Develop two or three bullet-point statements about the benefits the *participants* will get from achieving the session objective. This is the sales and marketing piece of the meeting prework and might take a bit of practice. How do these grand projects trickle down and impact your team day to day? How will their day-to-day work get easier, faster, better when this project is complete? That will get their attention. When you have their attention, you're closer to having their buy-in. When they understand what's happening, their role in making things happen, and the WIIFM, they will respond faster and perform at a higher level.

Saving the company millions/billions of dollars is not a compelling WIIFM. Figuring out how to store excess piping that crowds the shop floor, or reconfiguring the cubicles so the copy machine can be accessed easily by everyone, is.

By the end of this meeting/project:

(Insert the WIIFM based on the session objective. Here I'm using the copy machine sample objective.)

  The copy machine will be easier for everyone to access.
  There won't be congestion and confusion around the copy
    machine.
  You won't have to walk back and forth so often.

> *You'll get your copies faster/get more done faster/save lots*
>   *of time/*

If you aren't able to come up with two or three bullet points in your prework about why this session is of value, you're not ready to have this meeting and are setting the team up to waste their time.

Know your WIIFM before you begin.

ETR: Earn the Right

This is a short paragraph describing why you're qualified to facilitate this group. This isn't about your technical expertise—it's about your facilitation experience. Using the ETR script is optional after your first meeting with each team.

> *Since we're going to be spending the next (hours, days, year)*
>   *together, would it be okay if I told you a bit about myself? I've*
>   *been facilitating teams since…*

And/or:

> *I've had intensive training in facilitation, and I will apply the*
>   *skills learned in that training to guide us in successfully*
>   *accomplishing our session objective.*

End with:

> *I'm so glad to be here with you today because we're going to*
>   *accomplish…*

You'll agree this is so much more powerful than somebody getting up there saying, "I've never done this. I hope you'll cut me some slack." (Cue the hungry hyenas!)

Read These Charts

Now walk to the wall where the five pillars are posted.

1. Session Objective

Read the session objective.

2. Agenda

Read the agenda. There won't be times on the agenda, and you don't need to add any in your verbal review.

3. Agreements

Agreements are the ways we agree to work with each other while we're in this meeting to keep us on track and focused.

Respect the Speaker

> *Respect the speaker. One speaker at a time. Common courtesy. We can all do that, yes?* (Everybody says YES!)
>
> *HMOY have ever had people whisper at your meeting? The funny thing about the whisperers is they don't think anybody can hear them, because they're whispering. When really, everybody can hear it. It can be distracting, and I know we don't want to waste any time. How about we agree that we'll hold whispering?*
>
> *Instead, please put your hand up, or use a sticky note for your idea if you're not ready to share it with the whole group. We don't want to miss any of your ideas. Great, thank you.*

All Ideas Welcome

> *The more ideas, the more potential solutions. In fact, those "way out of the box" ideas often become the spark for solutions we may have never considered. So please, when you have an idea, put up your hand. Let's get all your ideas out here.*

Freedom to Disagree

> *With all these ideas out on the table, we may not agree with*
> *everything we hear. We can talk about anything when we do*
> *it in a respectful way. In my role as facilitator, I'll make sure*
> *we maintain a respectful, professional working environment.*
> *How's that sound?*

Start and End on Time

> *We'll start and end the meeting on time. I know that you're all*
> *busy and we don't want to waste a minute. So, we'll begin the*
> *meeting promptly as scheduled and end at* (time). *We will*
> *have a break every sixty to ninety minutes. We'll break at*
> (time) *for* (how long) *for lunch.*

Remember that starting and ending the meeting on time is an easy way to show respect and build trust. Don't reward dysfunctional behavior by waiting for late arrivals.

Electronics Off

> *HMOY have ever been at a meeting where cell phones and*
> *electronics have been distracting? Go ahead and check your*
> *electronics now and then please turn them off. Who here is an*
> *emergency point person? Someone who must be available no*
> *matter what? For those of you in that position, would you*
> *please turn your electronics to vibrate? If you do have to*
> *answer a call, please do that out in the hall. Thanks!*

4. Decision-Making Method: Consensus

> *It's important for us to know how we're going to make decisions
> in our meeting. I propose we use consensus as a method of
> making decisions.*

Ideally the method of decision-making was confirmed in the
prework already. In which case the script is as follows:

> *It was decided in the prework that we'll use consensus as our
> method to make decisions. Consensus means decision making
> through discussion rather than voting. Our definition listed
> here means:*
> • *I can live with that idea/decision and support it.*
> • *It does not mean: I think this is the best/only solution.*
>
> *It may mean that you can say, "While I don't love this idea, in
> listening to the other subject matter experts on the team, I am
> willing to support the decision. I recommend we closely track
> what happens in implementation of this decision to mitigate
> my concerns around…"*
> *Okay? So, when we get to a place in the meeting where we're
> going to make a decision, I propose we use consensus. How
> does that sound?*

You raise your hand. You will see nods, a quick hand raise, some
acknowledgment. And you will see some people do nothing, so include
this next question in your script.

> *If you did not respond, now and going forward, am I to assume
> you're in agreement?*

People usually say yes so you can wrap this up with an *Okay, thanks.*
Be sure to ask the question if everyone doesn't respond. I've been
facilitating a meeting, and after a long morning of presentations,
discussions, and clarifying questions and concerns, the team is finally

ready to say yes to a decision, and *then* a person speaks up and says, "You know, I didn't say yes back when we were talking about X before lunch. I'm not sure I'm on board with this whole idea."

Ka-boom. A huge anchor has been thrown overboard and with a jolt, the raft stops.

If you didn't ask, *"If you didn't respond, am I to assume you're in agreement?"* then you have no life preserver and the mess from the sabotage, innocent or not, is on you to clean up. If you did ask, you can say this:

> *I'm confused, I remember when we covered consensus we*
> *confirmed that, if you're not speaking up, that would be*
> *considered agreement. Tell me more about what's happening*
> *now?*

5. Parking Lot

> *The parking lot is a place to store ideas that might not be on the*
> *topic we're discussing at the time. And we don't want to lose*
> *any ideas, so we'll park them here. We'll make sure we decide*
> *what to do with them before the end of the meeting.*
> *These five agreements cover most anything we might encounter*
> *during our meeting. What else comes to mind that we might*
> *want to add for our team here, so we can do business*
> *effectively?*

Leave room at the bottom of the chart paper to add more if needed. Often people will ask for confidentiality (or Vegas rules) to be added, meaning that whatever is said in the room stays in the room. When the team asks for new agreements to be added, say, *How's that sound to everyone?*

You will have your markers ready to add agreements as necessary. Write them on the paper posted on the wall. However, the five agreements I use cover most dysfunctions you will encounter in your meetings and training sessions.

Cover the Logistics

Discuss the location of the bathrooms and exits, the temperature, and any other special instructions.

Team Introductions

Do team introductions if:

- They haven't been together before
- This is their first meeting as a new team
- A new member joins the team.

Keep it simple.

> *Let's meet everybody. This will be easy, team. We'll go round-robin. Take five to seven seconds and tell us:*
> - *Your name*
> - *Where you work*
> - *Your role on the project*
> - *A surprising fact about yourself*

When introductions are complete:

> *Great! Everyone, give your neighbor a high five and say, 'Glad you're here!'*

When you get to this point you will have completed the first agenda item: "welcome & overview."

> *Thanks, everybody. We're off to a great start. We just finished "welcome and overview", and now our next agenda item is...*

And that's the opening script. Rehearse it, stick to it, and you'll be set to facilitate a great meeting. Once the three steps to opening the session are complete—the setup, the kick off, and showtime—your heavy lifting is done. The context, *"how"* the work will be done, is set. Now it's over to the team, in their role as subject-matter experts, to complete the meeting objective.

THIRTY-FIVE

R.E.S.T

Have you ever been to a meeting and heard something like this?

"Okay so we agreed to X. Who is going to get this rolling? It looks like this could be your department, John."

John says, "Yeah, let me check on that. I'll get back to you."

And that's the last time we hear about what's happening with the decision the group spent hours on—until the next meeting, when John shares his regrets and apologies for not following up.

This happens all the time in meetings. Details fall through the cracks, teams are tired, and good intentions evaporate when we get to our busy desks and already-full plates.

Closing the session well is a gift to your team. This step solidifies action and expectations and is the key to maintaining momentum between meetings.

Make sure you build in time on your agenda to accomplish the steps below. Depending on the length and complexity of your meeting, you may need anywhere from five or thirty minutes to go through the closing activities.

Even after an hour-long meeting, you can feel drained. To make sure nothing gets missed use this four-step process that spells R-E-S-T.

- Review
- Evaluate
- Stream of actions
- Thank you and close.

Review

Do a quick look back at the work the team accomplished.

First, review the agenda.

- What was covered?
- What is left to cover?
- When will we cover the items that weren't covered?

Now take a look at all the action items. If decisions were made in your meeting, post another piece of chart paper on the wall titled "Actions."

- What action will be taken?
- Who is taking the action?
- How will they update the team? (What might the team need between meetings regarding this item? How will you update? Via email? If so, is there a current email roster?)
- When? When will the action be taken, and when will the team be updated? By close of business? This afternoon? (Include a date and time.)

Next, it's time to address accountability. This is the rubber-meets-the-road moment.

Team, what happens if we don't take action, and we don't do what we say we will do? It's been a nice session, but if nothing happens because of it, it means this meeting was a complete

waste of time. So, we will do whatever it takes to move the
ball, yes? Great! Thanks!

The "actions items" list from this meeting becomes an agenda item at your next meeting.

Next, you'll review the parking lot. Go through each item left and ask:

Have we covered it?
Do we need to cover it now?
When will we cover it?

Parking lot items can also become agenda items for the next meeting.

In some cases, a parking-lot item is taken by a team member and they carry out or investigate the item between now and the next meeting. If this happens, it becomes an action and is posted on the "action items" list.

Evaluation

I recommend handing out evaluation forms at all meetings, even those that are only an hour.

Doing an evaluation is the one way we can measure and continually improve our performance as meeting leaders so that we know what serves the group best. How can you know what worked and keep doing more of that if you don't get feedback? How can you learn what to fine tune without a vehicle through which the team can communicate with you? Both the good news and the news you can use from evaluation exercises are invaluable.

You'll notice the evaluation step isn't the last one in R-E-S-Ting your session. If you hand out the evaluation right before the team walks out the door, chances are you'll get less quality feedback. Even if they loved the meeting, they'll love moving on to the next thing more.

Stream of Actions

These are the little details that can slip through the cracks between meetings. Cover them now and save yourself the time it will take to chase these details down between meetings:

- Who has recorded the minutes and how will they be shared with the group?
- Who will collect and record the charts on the wall if the group has recorded work?
- When and where do we meet again?
- Who will be facilitating?
- Who needs to be there?
- What are we committed to accomplishing in the meantime?
- Who has a list of the email addresses and phone numbers of all the participants?

Thank You and Close

Remember to say thank you to the team. It's basic good manners, and that's what you want to be modeling.

- Let the participants know the session is officially over.
- Thank them for taking the time and energy to attend the meeting.
- Celebrate all wins. This could be as simple as, *Let's have a round of applause for your great work today*. Depending on the session, consider certificates and gifts to reward accomplishments.

Closing the session is really a thorough checklist to confirm everyone is on board and knows what happens next. Walk right down these lists of questions and you won't miss a thing. Then, go take a rest yourself. You deserve it!

THIRTY-SIX

It's a Wrap

I was training an Air Force team of process improvement practitioners. They were efficient, energized, and having a lot of success in their work. I was hearing the buzz about their leader, whom I would get to meet at lunch. He'd be presenting an achievement award to one of their teammates, a young airman transferring to a new assignment.

"Wait till you get to meet Major Black. He greets us on the flight line in the morning and says good bye at the end of day. He always makes sure we've got what we need and helps us find a way through problems—just a great guy."

When Major Black came into the room, the team popped out of their chairs to attention. This wasn't necessary protocol and a huge sign of respect. Smiling and excited, he arrived early, which gave him time to greet and talk individually with members of his team. He had prepared notes for the occasion.

"We're here to honor Tyler today. His great work has allowed us all to be successful. Tyler got me thinking about 'componency'. We're all components, like Legos. There is no top or bottom on our team. I cannot form and take shape, without the people around me. We cannot become something bigger without each other to lock into. Like Legos, at our base, we're open and ready to receive ideas and knowledge. The bumps at the top, our heads, allow us to connect with our teammates. We're smooth on our sides, coming together without friction, letting things that do not serve us slide off. And in doing so, we become stronger together. We honor Tyler's 'componency' here today —his ability to serve the team with his intelligence, experience and caring. I'm so proud to have worked with and learned from him."

Wow. I was ready to re-enlist. I wanted to be on that team. I saw the looks of admiration and love (yes, love!) from the team for this leader. He had taken the time to prepare a story about this young man and about his team. He was on time, energized, prepared, focused. All the qualities of great leadership. His energy and attitude were contagious, and the results showed. I was witnessing a great leader in action, an accumulation of many little things.

How you do anything is how you do everything.

Great Meetings = Great Leaders

Now that you've been through all the steps of how to make your meetings great, let's compare how great leaders approach the role (to produce great meetings) with how the untrained or overwhelmed leader will approach the role (to produce meetings that suck).

A Leader of Great Meetings

> *Books planning time weekly to do prework for meetings.*
> *Does prework—sets aside planning time for meetings for the week: What is the session objective for the meeting? Why are we here? What will we accomplish?*
> *What's the agenda and/or the steps to accomplish the session objective?*
> *Opens the session with energy and organization (see the five pillars).*
> *Asks open-ended questions that increase discussion and participation. They begin with "what," "how," and "why."*

Listens and makes eye contact, waits until person is done talking to speak.

Keeps energy up. Is optimistic and open. Says yes to ideas: "Let's talk more about that…"

Starts and ends on time.

Has the tools and skills to respectfully manage dysfunctional behavior.

Keeps and reviews the parking lot items.

Creates action plan before ending the meeting: who is doing what, by when?

Follows up and communicates. Updates and stays in touch as actions from meeting are implemented between meetings.

A Leader of Meetings That Suck

Accepts invites to multiple meetings that begin at the same time and shows up late for the one they choose to attend.

Leaves people waiting at the two other meetings.

Doesn't follow up with the leaders of the missed meetings.

Doesn't take time to consider why the meeting is taking place, and asks the team to bring them up to speed: "So, what do we want to talk about?"

Can't hide they are unprepared. This sends the message, "This meeting is not really important."

Excuses include: "I'm a seat-of-the-pants kind of person." "Geez, I really didn't think about what to say… Uh, glad you're here. Hope this will be worthwhile."

Asks closed-ended questions: Anything else? Anyone have problems with this idea? Are you ready to move on?

Interrupts and doesn't make eye contact.

Has low energy. Is closed-minded. "No, that won't work." Tells people what to do, talks about their opinion and why it's best. "That idea will never work and here's why…" "No, we could never do that, we tried that before and it won't fly. Here's what we should do…"

*Ends meetings late (often accompanied by lame excuses: "I really
     want to respect your time, so I won't keep you too much
     longer.")*

*Condescends, calls people out, shuts down conversations,
     interrupts, embarrasses people in front of the team. Gets loud,
     has no agreements—or calls them "ground rules" and doesn't
     create a context in which to use them.*

*Doesn't have a parking lot chart, or has one and doesn't use it—
     throws it in the garbage; all ideas lost, along with trust and
     respect.*

*Doesn't solidify actions: "Okay so someone will get back to us on
     that? Right?" No date, no action outlined.*

*Doesn't follow up on meeting minutes or action plans. Ideas from
     the meeting are lost or not moved forward.*

It's a shame how many great ideas are lost in the muck of meetings
that suck. How thousands upon thousands of hours of people's lives,
hours they can never get back, are lost in unproductive meetings. How
the hurt and heartache caused by dysfunctional behavior is left
unchecked.

Now you have the information you need to understand why meetings suck and you know what to do about it. You know how and why
organizational performance is directly tied to meeting performance.
You know there are financial, cultural, and operational consequences
of bad meetings. And you know that your professional reputation is at
stake. You know the common blind spots that keep bad meetings in
place. Meetings that suck are a result of missing some easy steps you
may have not known about before.

Being a great facilitator is a core competency of great leaders, and
that takes training and practice.

Doing your prework is essential.

You've got your prework to-do list ready on the side of your desk,
and you're well set up to clarify the session objective, appropriately
handle the sales and marketing of your meeting, pick your A-team,

send advance invites and welcome emails, and devote time in advance to logistics

The five pillars of great meetings are familiar to you now, and you no longer start a meeting you're leading without clarifying the session objective, the agenda, the agreements, the decision-making methods, and the parking lot.

Continue to practice. Be sure to become a master of the open-ended question, which will always start with *what, how,* or *why.* The open-ended question is your go-to super-facilitator tool!

Rehearse the scripts for addressing dysfunctional behavior with the T-E-A-M approach out loud in front of a mirror. Remember to smile.

The time you put into your own training and development will serve you well.

Begin by booking a meeting with yourself, one hour per week, to go over the tools in this book. Then book another one-hour block per week to begin doing prework for meetings you have coming up. You will start to notice the time you're saving by doing this kind of planning.

———

Meetings are a petri dish of how your organization functions. Watch what happens to organizational performance when you implement these tools and your meetings become hubs for creativity and innovation. Over time, watch your organization's culture shift to one that's more healthy, robust, and engaged. Financial performance will improve, staff morale will increase, turnover rates will decline, and facilitation skills will become part of regular training and development programs for your leadership and management teams. Expanding your emotional intelligence while using these field-tested tools will reinvigorate people. They will feel their gifts and talents are valued and honored. People change when they are treated with respect. Seeing this happen is one of the gifts and joys of my work.

Imagine standing at the front of the meeting room. Chart paper and sticky notes containing lists, ideas and actions cover the walls, telling the story of the last two days of meetings and team success.

Music is still humming in the background. Little green, orange, and blue Play-Doh sculptures are dotted around the U-shaped table. Peppermint wrappers, cups, and cookie crumbs along with handouts from two PowerPoint presentations are strewn along the tables. You smile as you look at the personalized name tents. Jason crossed out his name and called himself "Spiderman."

A few small groups are still in the room, smiling, laughing, and looking at the work laid out on the walls. Several people come over to you.

"Wow, we never *ever*, thought we'd be at this point today. Thank you for all you did to keep us on track and get this work done!"

It was a challenging session objective this team took on, with lots of data to sift through and decisions to be made that would impact many people and potentially change major procedures. Despite initial apprehension about what appeared to be opposing sides, bridges were built, compromises made, and action plans set in motion.

After all your hours of prework, handling logistics, finding the A-team, practicing open-ended questions, and rehearsing the showtime and T-E-A-M scripts, the meeting was a great success.

This can be your meeting. Keep practicing. This will be your meeting.

That is my wish for you.

I know we can change the world—one meeting at a time.

Acknowledgments

What a TEAM!

A standing ovation and sincere thanks to Chris Flett, my business coach, for your valued counsel, humor and patience. You leave people, including me, better than you find them. And to Boni Wagner-Stafford, the Book Whisperer, whose exceptional generosity of time and talent skillfully turned my manuscript into a book. Your commitment made the book real. Your energy made the process fun!

About Peg Drummond

Peg Drummond is founder of the business and leadership success consulting firm *Super Teams*. Having facilitated and trained teams around the globe for over two decades, Peg is a respected coach and consultant. She is known for focus, high energy, and ability to motivate teams and people to create powerful strategies for taking action, changing culture, and achieving results. She works with leaders in private industry and the public sector and helps them focus on innovation and creativity, and as a result, processes are improved and trust and respect are built.

Super Teams' mission is transforming organizations and the people in them by creating environments of trust and respect that improve performance, and heal the workplace and the world.

Changing the world, one meeting at a time.

www.superteams.com
peg@superteams.com